Berlitz®

Hindi

phrase book & dictionary

Berlitz Publishing
New York   London   Singapore

Contacting the Editors
Every effort has been made to provide accurate information in this publication, but changes are inevitable. The publisher cannot be responsible for any resulting loss, inconvenience or injury. We would appreciate it if readers would call our attention to any errors or outdated information. We also welcome your suggestions; if you come across a relevant expression not in our phrase book, please contact us at: **comments@berlitzpublishing.com**

All Rights Reserved
© 2007 Berlitz Publishing/APA Publications (UK) Ltd.
Berlitz Trademark Reg. U.S. Patent Office and other countries. Marca Registrada. Used under license from Berlitz Investment Corporation.

Eleventh Printing: January 2014
Printed in China

Senior Commissioning Editor: Kate Drynan
Design: Beverley Speight
Translation: updated by Wordbank
Phonetic transcription: Wordbank
Production Manager: Vicky Glover
Picture Researcher: Beverley Speight
Cover Photos: © APA Julian Love & istockphoto

Interior Photos: APA Julian Love p.1,12,27,28,31,54,56,58,59,60,61,62,63,64,68,70,73,74,75 76,78,779,85,98,101,102,106,108,110,111,112,113,115,117,119,123,125,126,129,131,135, 140,170; istockphoto p.14,16,21,25,35,36,41,45,47,51,52,65,66,69,72,77,81,83,84,89,91,92 94,95,97,121,132,137,138,139,147,148,151,153,154,156,157,159,161; APA Britta Jachinski p.43; APA Bev Speight p.49,173; APA Corrie Wingate p.88,96; APA Lydia Evans p.90; APA Nikt Wong p.86; APA Peter Stuckings p/93; APA Gregory Wrona p.133.

Contents

Food & Drink

People

Leisure Time

Special Requirements

Contents

6

In an Emergency

Dictionary

Pronunciation

This section is designed to make you familiar with the sounds of Hindi using our simplified phonetic transcription. You'll find the pronunciation of the Hindi letters and sounds explained below, together with their "imitated" equivalents. This system is used throughout the phrase book; simply read the pronunciation as if it were English, noting any special rules below.

Hindi is written in the Devanagari script. Similar to other Indian languages, the alphabets of Devanagari script are grouped based on their pronunciation. The first 11 letters are grouped as vowels. The vowels are organized in the sequence of a short vowel followed by the long counterpart, followed by a string of consonants.

Vowels

All the vowels are in two versions in the script: full vowel and vowel sign. The vowel signs are used when a vowel is followed by a consonant. If a vowel precedes another vowel or if a word begins with a vowel, the full vowel is used. The vowel signs are written next to the preceding consonant. The vowel signs can be written before, after, below and above the consonant. It can also appear without the sign at all. 'a' is assumed wherever there is no indication of a vowel sign. While the vowel signs are much simpler to master than the full vowels, the pronunciation of both versions is the same.

Consonants

Hindi consonants are divided into five groups depending on their articulation. Each group has five letters (sounds) and these letters or sounds are further divided into three subgroups – voiced, unvoiced and nasal.

If two or more consonants are adjoined, the consonants are not written in full. They are merged together to form a new symbol. Please note that some of these symbols can be easily recognized while others look vastly different.

Hindi uses punctuation marks in a similar way as English, with one notable exception - the period or full stop. This is represented by a vertical line | .

Vowels & Diphthongs

a	अ	*like **u** in r**u**n*
	आ	*like **a** in f**a**ther*
i	इ	*like **i** in h**i**t*
	ई	*like **e** in t**ee**th*
u	उ	*like **u** in p**u**t*
	ऊ	*like **oo** in c**oo**l*
e	ए	*like **e** in th**e**y*
ei	ऐ	*like **a** in c**a**re*
o	ओ	*like **o** in b**o**th*
au	औ	*like **ou** in **ou**ch*
ri	ऋ	*like **ri** in K**ri**shna*

Consonants

g	ग	*like the **g** in **g**et, **g**un, mu**g**, **g**ive*
gh	घ	*make a **g** and **h** sound and run them together like **g**+**h***
n	न	*like the **in** in s**ing**, w**ing**, br**ing***
ch	च	*like the **ch** in mu**ch**, su**ch***
chh	छ	*add an extra **h** sound to the end of **ch** sound **ch**+**h***
jh	झ	*make a **j** and **h** sound and run them together like **j**+**h***
t	त	*like the **t** in **t**ree, **t**ea*
d	द	*like the **d** in **d**ay, **d**o, **d**eed*
dh	ध	*make a hard **d** and **h** sound and run them together like **d**+**h***

th	थ	*like the th in thin, both*
sh	ष	*like the sh in she, show, shop*
s	स	*like the s in seen, sun*

Hindi is the official language of India and it is also the most widely spoken vernacular in the forms of different dialects. Hindi has a strong standing in the north of India but it is not widely spoken in the south and it bears little relation to the languages spoken there. It is the official language for the states of Bihar, Haryana, Himachal, Pradesh, Madhya, Pradesh, Rajasthan and Uttar Pradesh. It is also spoken in Surinam, Mauritius and Fiji.

How to use this Book

Sometimes you see two alternatives separated by a slash. Choose the one that's right for your situation.

ESSENTIAL

I'm on vacation/
business.

मैं छुट्टी/व्यवसाय पर हूं।
Main chhutti/vyavsay par hoon.

I'm going to...

मैं...के लिए जा रहा हूं।
Main... ke liye ja raha hoon.

I'm staying at
the...Hotel.

मैं...होटल में ठहर रहा हूं।
Main... hotel men thahar raha hoon.

Words you may see are shown in YOU MAY SEE boxes.

YOU MAY SEE...

सीमा शुल्क	customs
शुल्क-मुक्त वस्तुएं	duty-free goods
घोषित करने के लिए वस्तुएं	goods to declare

Any of the words or phrases listed can be plugged into the sentence below.

Tickets

A...ticket.

एक...टिकट *ek... ticket.*

   one-way

एक-तरफ *ek-taraf*

   round-trip [return]

वापसी यात्रा *vapasi yatra*

   first class

फर्स्ट क्लास *first class*

   economy class

बिजनेस क्लास *business class*

Hindi phrases appear in purple.

Read the simplified pronunciation as if it were English. For more on pronunciation, see page 7.

Taxi & Rickshaw

Can you send a taxi?

क्या आप एक टैक्सी भेज सकते हैं?
kya aap ek taxi bhej sakte hain?

Do you have the number for a taxi?

क्या आपके पास टैक्सी के लिए नंबर है?
kya aapke paas taxi ke liye number hai?

I'd like a taxi now/ for tomorrow at...

मैं अभी/कल के लिए...पर टैक्सी चाहूंगा / चाहूंगी *main abhi/kal ke liye...par taxi chahoonga m / chahoongi f*

For Asking Directions, see page 33.

Related phrases can be found by going to the page number indicated.

When different gender forms apply, the masculine form is followed by *m*; feminine by *f*.

Hindi uses numerous English loan words, which makes it easy for English speakers to build their vocabulary quickly. Note though that the pronunciation of many of the loan words is different in Hindi.

Information boxes contain relevant country, culture and language tips.

Expressions you may hear are shown in You May Hear boxes.

YOU MAY HEAR...

कृपया, केवल नकद दें।
kripya, keval nakad dein

Cash only, please.

Color-coded side bars identify each section of the book.

Survival

Arrival & Departure

ESSENTIAL

I'm on vacation [holiday]/business.	मैं छुट्टी/व्यवसाय पर हूं। *Main chhutti/vyavsay par hoon.*
I'm going to...	मैं...के लिए जा रहा हूं। *Main... ke liye ja raha hoon.*
I'm staying at the...Hotel.	मैं...होटल में ठहर रहा हूं। *Main... hotel men thahar raha hoon.*

YOU MAY HEAR...

कृपया, आपका पासपोर्ट। *Kripya, aapka passport.*	Your passport, please.
आपकी यात्रा का प्रयोजन क्या है? *Aapki yatra ka prayojan kya hai?*	What's the purpose of your visit?
आप कहां ठहर रहे हैं? *Aap kahan thahar rahe hain?*	Where are you staying?
आप कितने समय तक ठहर रहे हैं? *Aap kitne samay tak thahar rahe hain?*	How long are you staying?
यहां आप किसके साथ हैं? *Yahan aap kiske saath hain?*	Who are you with?

Border Control

I'm just passing through.	मैं बस गुजर रहा हूं। *Main bas guzar raha hoon.*
I'd like to declare	मैं करना चाहता हूं... *Main ghoshit karna chahta hoon...*
I have nothing to declare.	मेरे पास घोषित करने के लिए कुछ नहीं है। *Mere pas ghoshit karne ke liye kuchh nahin hai.*

YOU MAY HEAR...

घोषित करने के लिए कुछ है?   Anything to declare?
Ghoshit karne ke liye kuchh hai?

आपको शुल्क देना चाहिए ।   You must pay duty.
Aapko shulk dena chahiye?

इस बैग को खोलें।   Open this bag
Is bag ko kholen.

YOU MAY SEE...

सीमा शुल्क	customs
शुल्क-मुक्त वस्तुएं	duty-free goods
घोषित करने के लिए वस्तुएं	goods to declare
घोषित करने के लिए कुछ नहीं	nothing to declare
पासपोर्ट नियंत्रण	passport control
पुलिस	police

Money

ESSENTIAL

Where's...?	...कहां है? ... *kahan hai?*
the ATM	एटीएम *ATM*
the bank	बैंक *Bank*
the currency exchange office	मुद्रा विनिमय कार्यालय *mudra vinimay karyalay*
What time does the bank open/close?	बैंक कब खुलता/बंद होता हैं? *Bank kab khulta/band hota hai?*
I'd like to change some dollars/pounds/euros into Rupees.	मैं डॉलर/पाउंड स्टर्लिंग/यूरो को रुपये में बदलना चाहता / चाहती हूं। *Main dollar/pount sterling/euro ko rupaye men badalna chahta m / chahti f hoon.*
I want to cash some traveler's checks [cheques].	मैं यात्री चेक को भुनाना चाहता / चाहती हूं। *Main yatri cheque bhunana chahta m / chahti f hoon.*

When exchanging money, do not accept ripped or dirty notes as you may struggle to use them at a later stage. Also, remember that large denominations (anything over Rs100) may also be difficult to use, especially in smaller stores as they often do not have the change.

At the Bank

I'd like to change money/get a cash advance.	मैं मुद्रा को बदलना/नकद अग्रिम प्राप्त करना चाहता / चाहती हूं। *Main mudra ko badalana/ nakad agrim prapt karna chahta m / chahti f hoon.*

What's the exchange rate/fee?	विनिमय दर/शुल्क क्या है? *Vinimay dar/shulk kya hai?*
I think there's a mistake.	मैं सोचता हूं कि कोई गलती हुई है। *Main sochata hoon ki koi galati hui hai.*
I lost my traveler's cheques.	मैंने अपने यात्री चेक खो दिए *Maine apane yatri cheque Kho diye.*
My card...	मेरा कार्ड... *Mera card...*
was lost	खो गया *kho gaya*
was stolen	चोरी हो गया *chori ho gaya*
doesn't work	काम नहीं करता है *kam nahin karta hai*
The ATM ate my card.	मेरा कार्ड एटीएम में फंस गया। *Mera card ATM mein fans gaya.*

For Numbers, see page 165.

YOU MAY SEE...

कार्ड यहां डालें।	insert card here
रद्द करें।	cancel
क्लीयर करें।	clear
प्रवेश करें।	enter
पिन	PIN
निकासी	withdraw
चेकिंग [चालू] खाते से	from checking [current] account
बचत खाते से	from savings account
रसीद	receipt

YOU MAY SEE...

The official currency is the Rupee (Rs), divided into 100 paise (p).
Coins: 1, 2, 5 Rs and 5, 10, 20, 25, 50 paise
Notes: 5, 10, 20, 50, 100, 500, 1000

Getting Around

ESSENTIAL

How do I get to town?	मैं शहर तक कैसे पहुंच सकता / सकती हूं?
	Main shahar tak kaise pahoonch sakta m / sakti f hoon?
Where's...?	...कहां है? *...kahan hai?*
the airport	हवाई अड्डा *hawai adda*
the train station	ट्रेन स्टेशन *train station*
the bus station	बस स्टेशन *bus station*
the subway station [underground] station	सबवे स्टेशन [अंडरग्राउंड] *subway [underground]* स्टेशन *station*
Is it far from here?	क्या यह यहां से दूर है?
	kya yah yahan se dur hai?
Where do I buy a ticket?	मैं टिकट कहां से खरीदूं?
	Main ticket kahan se kharidun?
A one-way/ return-trip ticket to...	...के लिए एक-तरफ/वापसी यात्रा टिकट
	... ke liye ek-taraf/vaapsi ticket
How much?	कितना? *kitna?*
Which gate/line?	कौन-सा गेट/लाइन?
	kaun-sa gate/line?
Which platform?	कौन-सा प्लेटफॉर्म?
	kaun-sa platform?
Where can I get a taxi?	मैं कहां से टैक्सी पा सकता हूं?
	Main kahan se taxi pa sakta hoon?
Take me to this address.	मुझे इस पते पर ले चलो।
	Mujhe is pate par le chalo.
Can I have a map?	क्या मुझे मानचित्र मिल सकता है?
	Kya mujhe manchitra mil sakta hai?

Tickets

When's...to ...?	...के लिए...कब है?	... ke liye...kab hai?
the (first) bus	(पहली) बस	(pahli) bus
the (next) flight	(अगली) उड़ान	(agli) udan
the (last) train	(अंतिम) ट्रेन	(antim) train
Where do I buy a ticket?	मैं टिकट कहां से खरीदूं?	
		Main ticket kahan se kharidun?
One/Two ticket(s) please.	कृपया, एक/दो टिकट दें।	
		Kripya ek/do ticket den.
For today/tomorrow.	आज/कल के लिए	Aaj/kal ke liye.
A...ticket.	एक...टिकट	ek... ticket.
one-way	एक-तरफ	ek-taraf
return trip	वापसी यात्रा	vapasi yatra
first class	फर्स्ट क्लास	first class
business class	बिजनेस क्लास	business class
economy class	इकोनॉमी क्लास	economy class
How much?	कितना?	kitna?
Is there a discount for...?	...के लिए क्या कोई छूट है?	
		...ke liye kya koi chhut hai?
children	बच्चे	bachche
students	छात्र	chhatra
senior citizens	वरिष्ठ नागरिक	varishtha nagarik
tourists	पर्यटक	paryatak
The express bus/ express train, please.	कृपया, एक्सप्रेस बस/एक्सप्रेस ट्रेन।	
		kripya, express bus/ express train.
The local bus/train, please.	कृपया, स्थानीय बस/ट्रेन	kripya, sthaniya bus/train.
I have an e-ticket.	मेरे पास ई-टिकट है।	mere pas e-ticket hai.
Can I buy...	क्या मैं...खरीद सकता / सकती हूं	
		kya main... kharid sakta **m** / sakti **f** hoon?

a ticket on the bus/train?	बस/ट्रेन पर एक टिकट *bus/train par ek ticket*
the ticket before boarding?	बोर्डिंग से पहले टिकट *boarding se pahle ticket?*
How long is this ticket valid?	यह टिकट कितने समय तक मान्य है? *yah ticket kitne samay tak manya hai?*
Can I return on the same ticket?	क्या मैं उसी टिकट पर लौट सकता / सकती हूं? *kya main usi ticket par laut sakta m / sakti f hoon?*
I'd like to... my reservation.	मैं... के लिए अपना आरक्षण चाहता / चाहती हूं। *Main... ke liye arakshan chahta m / chahti f hoon.*
cancel	रद्द *radda*
change	बदलाव *badlav*
confirm	पुष्ट *pushta*

For Days, see page 167.

Plane

Airport Transfer

How much is a taxi to the airport?	हवाई अड्डे के लिए टैक्सी कितना लेती है? *Hawai adde ke liye taxi kitna leti hai?*
To...Airport, please.	कृपया...हवाई अड्डे के लिए। *kripya...hawai adde ke liye.*
My airline is...	मेरी एयरलाइन...है *Meri airline... hai.*
My flight leaves at...	मेरी उड़ान...पर निकलती है। *Meri udan... par nikalti hai.*
I'm in a rush.	मैं जल्दी में हूं। *Main jaldi men hoon.*
Can you take an alternate route?	क्या आप वैकल्पिक मार्ग ले सकते हैं? *Kya aap vaikalpik marg le sakte hain?*
Can you drive faster/slower?	क्या आप तेज/धीमे चला सकते हैं? *Kya aap tez/dhimen chala sakte hai?*

For Time, see page 167.

YOU MAY HEAR...

आप किस एयरलाइन में जा रहे हैं?
Aap kis airline men ja rahe hai.

घरेलू या अंतर्राष्ट्रीय
gharelu ya antarrashtriya

कौन सा टर्मिनल? *kaun sa terminal?*

What airline
are you flying?

Domestic or International?

What terminal?

YOU MAY SEE...

आगमन	arrivals
प्रस्थान	departures
सामान का दावा	baggage claim
सुरक्षा	security
घरेलू उड़ानें	domestic flights
अंतर्राष्ट्रीय उड़ानें	international flights
चेक-इन	check-in desk
ई-टिकट चेक-इन	e-ticket check-in
प्रस्थान गेट	departure gates

Checking In

Where's check-in?	चेक-इन कहां है?	*check-in kahan hai?*
My name is. . .	मेरा नाम. . .है।	*mera nam . . . hai*
I'm going to. . .	मैं. . .के लिए जा रहा / रही हूं।	
		*main. . . ke lie ja raha **m** / rahi **f** hoon*
I have. . .	मेरे पास. . .है।	*mere pas. . . hai*
one suitcase	एक सूटकेस	*ek suitcase*
two suitcases	दो सूटकेस	*do suitcase*
one piece	एक पीस	*ek piece*
How much luggage is allowed?	कितने लगेज की अनुमति है?	*kitne luggage ki anumati hai?*
Is that pounds or kilos?	क्या वह पाउंड या किलो है?	*kya vah pound ya kilo hai?*
Which terminal?	किस टर्मिनल?	*kis terminal?*
Which gate?	कौन-सा गेट?	*kaun-sa gate?*
I'd like a window/ an aisle seat.	मैं खिड़की/गलियारे की सीट चाहूंगा / चाहूंगी।	
		*Main khidaki/galiyare ki seat chahoonga **m** / chahoongi **f**.*
When do we leave/arrive?	हम कब निकलेंगे/पहुंचेंगे?	
		Ham kab niklenge/pahoonchenge?
Is the flight delayed?	क्या उड़ान में विलंब है?	*kya udan men vilamb hai?*
How late?	कितनी देरी?	*kitani deri?*

Luggage

Where is/are. . .?	. . .कहां है/हैं?	*. . .kahan hai@hain?*
the luggage trolleys	लगेज ट्रॉली	*luggage trolley*
the luggage lockers	लगेज लॉकर	*luggage locker*
the baggage claim	बैगेज क्लेम	*baggage claim*
My luggage has been lost/stolen.	मेरा लगेज खो गया/चुरा लिया गया है।	
		Mera luggage kho gaya/chura liya gaya hai.
My suitcase is damaged.	मेरा सूटकेस क्षतिग्रस्त हो गया है।	
		Mera suitcase kshatigrasta ho gaya hai.

YOU MAY HEAR...

अगला! *agla!*	Next!
कृपया, अपना पासपोर्ट/टिकट दें। *kripya apna passport/ticket den.*	Your ticket/passport, please.
क्या आप कोई सामान लेकर प्रवेश कर रहे हैं? *kya aap koi saman lekar pravesh kar rahe hain?*	Are you checking any luggage?
वह साथ ले जाने के लिए बहुत भारी है [हैंड लगेज का पीस] *Vah sath le jane ke liye bahut bhari hai [hand luggage ka piece].*	That's too large for a carry-on [piece of hand luggage].
क्या ये बैग आपने स्वयं से पैक किये हैं? *kya ye bag aapne swayam se pack kiye hain.*	Did you pack these bags yourself?
क्या किसी ने तुम्हें कुछ ले जाने के लिए दिया? *kya kisi ne tumhe kuch le jane ke liye diya?*	Did anyone give you anything to carry?
अपने जूते निकाल लें। *Apne joote nikal len.*	Take off your shoes.
अब चढ़ रहे हैं... *ab chad rahe hain...*	Now boarding...

Finding your Way

Where is/are...?	...कहां है/हैं? ... *kahan hai/hain?*
the currency exchange	मुद्रा विनिमय *mudra vinimay*
the car hire	किराये की कार *kiraye ki car*
the exit	निकास *nikas*
the taxis	टैक्सी *Taxi*
Is there...	क्या कोई... *kya koi...*
into town?	शहर को जाती है? *shahar ko jati hai?*
a bus	एक बस *bus*
a train	एक ट्रेन *ek train*
a Metro	एक मेट्रो *ek metro*

For Asking Directions, see page 33.

For comprehensive information on train timetables, routes, fares and availability, visit Indian Railways website at **www.indianrail.gov.in.** Porters at railway stations expect to be tipped around Rs20 a bag.

For long waits inbetween trains, retiring rooms will take in passengers with valid travel tickets or passes. Booking in advance is possible.

Train

Where's the train station?	ट्रेन स्टेशन कहां है?	*train station kahan hai?*
How far is it?	वह कितनी दूर है?	*vah kitni door hai?*
Where is/are...?	...कहां है?	*...kahan hai?*
the ticket office	टिकट कार्यालय	*ticket kaaryalaya*
the information desk	सूचना डेस्क	*soochna desk*
the luggage lockers	लगेज लॉकर	*luggage locker*
the platforms	प्लेटफॉर्म	*platform*
Can I have a schedule [timetable]?	क्या मुझे शेड्यूल [टाइमटेबल] मिल सकता है?	*kya mujhe schedule [timetable] mil sakta hai?*

YOU MAY SEE...

प्लेटफॉर्म	platforms
सूचना	information
आरक्षण	reservations
प्रतीक्षा कक्ष	waiting room
आगमन	arrivals
प्रस्थान	departures

How long is the trip?	यात्रा कितनी लंबी है?	*yaatra kitni lambi hai?*
Is it a direct train?	क्या यह सीधी ट्रेन है?	*kya yah sidhi train hai?*
Do I have to change trains?	क्या मुझे ट्रेनें बदलनी होंगी?	*kya mujhe trainein badalni hongi?*
Is the train on time?	क्या ट्रेन समय पर है?	*kya train samay par hai?*

For Tickets, see page 19.

Departures

Which track [platform] to...?	...के लिए कौन सा ट्रैक [प्लेटफार्म] है?
	...ke liye kaun sa platform hai
Is this the track [platform]/ train to...?	क्या...के लिए यह ट्रैक [प्लेटफार्म] /ट्रेन है?
	kya...ke liye yah track [platform]/train hai
Where is track [platform]...?	ट्रैक [प्लेटफार्म]...कहां है?
	track [platform]...kahan hai
Where do I change for...?	मैं...के लिए कहां बदलूं?
	main...ke liye kahan badaloon

On Board

Can I sit here/open the window?	क्या मैं यहां बैठ/खिड़की खोल सकता / सकती हूं?
	*kya main yahan baith/khidki khol sakta **m** / sakti **f** hoon?*

YOU MAY HEAR...

कृपया, टिकट दें। *kripya, ticket dein*   Tickets, please.
आपको ....पर बदलना है। *aapko...par badalna hai*   You have to change at...
अगला स्टॉप...है। *agla stop...hai*   Next stop...

That's my seat.   वह मेरी सीट है। *vah meri seat hai*
Here's my reservation.   यह मेरा आरक्षण है। *yah mera aarakshan hai*

Bus

Where's the bus station?	बस स्टेशन कहां है?	*bus station kahan hai?*
How far is it?	वह कितनी दूर है?	*vah kitni door hai?*
How do I get to...?	मैं...के लिए कैसे जा सकता हूं?	*main...ke liye kaise jaa sakta hoon?*
Is this the bus to...?	क्या यह...को जाने वाली बस है?	*kya yah...ko jaane wali bus hai?*
Can you tell me when to get off?	क्या आप मुझे बता सकते हैं कि कब उतरना है?	*kya aap mujhe bata sakte hain ki kab utarna hai?*
Do I have to change buses?	क्या मुझे बसें बदलनी हैं?	*kya mujhe busein badalni hain?*
Stop here, please!	कृपया, यहां रोकें!	*Kripya, yahan rokein*

For Tickets, see page 19.

YOU MAY SEE...

बस स्टॉप	bus stop
अनुरोध स्टॉप	request stop
प्रवेश/निकास	entrance/exit
अपने टिकट पर मुहर लगाए	stamp your ticket

The extensive bus system connects virtually every part of the country. Services range from clapped-out old rust buckets on more rural routes to deluxe, state-of-the-art air-conditioned express coaches on major highways. In cities, it is often easier to catch a rickshaw or taxi than try to figure out which buses go where.

Metro

Where's the metro station?	मेट्रो स्टेशन कहां है? *metro station kahan hai?*
A map, please.	कृपया, एक मानचित्र दें। *kripya, ek maanchitra dein*
Which line for...?	...के लिए कौन सी लाइन? *...ke liye kaun si line?*
Which direction?	कौन सी दिशा? *kaun si disha?*
Do I have to transfer [change]?	क्या मुझे स्थानांतरण [बदलने] की आवश्यकता है? *kya mujhe sthanantran badalne ki aavashyakta hai?*
Is this the metro to...?	क्या यह...को जाने वाली मेट्रो है? *kya yah...ko jaane wali metro hai?*
How many stops to...?	...के लिए कितने स्टॉप? *...ke liye kitne stop?*
Where are we?	हम कहां हैं? *hum kahan hain?*

For Tickets, see page 19.

Boat & Ferry

When is the ferry/ riverboat to...?	...के लिए फेरी/ नाव कब है?
	...ke liye ferry/naav kab hai?
What time is the next sailing/ crossing?	अगली नौकायन/पार लगाने का समय कब है?
	agli naukaayan/paar lagane ka samaya kab hai?
Can I book a seat/ cabin?	क्या मैं एक सीट/केबिन बुक कर सकता हूं?
	kya main ek seat/cabin book kar sakta hoon?
How long is the crossing?	कॉसिंग कितनी दूर है?
	crossing kitni door hai?

For Tickets, see page 19.

YOU MAY SEE...

लाइफ बोट	life boats
लाइफ जैकेट	life jackets

Apart from river ferries, there are very few boat services in India. The Andaman Islands are connected to Kolkata, Chennai and Vishakapatnam by boat, and to each other. Kerala has a regular passenger boat system. There are also luxury river cruises along the Brahmaputra and Ganges, run by the Assam Bengal navigation Company (**www.assambengalnavigation.com**).

Taxi & Rickshaw

Where can I get a taxi?	मुझे एक टैक्सी कहां से मिल सकती है? *mujhe ek taxi kahan se mil sakti hai?*
Can you send a taxi?	क्या आप एक टैक्सी भेज सकते हैं? *kya aap ek taxi bhej sakte hain?*
Do you have the number for a taxi?	क्या आपके पास टैक्सी के लिए नंबर है? *kya aapke paas taxi ke liye number hai?*
I'd like a taxi now/ for tomorrow at...	मैं अभी/कल के लिए...पर टैक्सी चाहूंगा / चाहूंगी। *main abhi/kal ke liye...par taxi chahoonga m / chahoongi f*
Pick me up at...	मुझे...बजे उठा लें। *mujhe...baje utha lein*
I'm going to...	मैं...के लिए जा रहा हूं। *main...ke liye jaa raha hoon*
this address	यह पता *yah pata*
the airport	हवाई अड्डा *hawai adda*
the train station	ट्रेन स्टेशन *train station*
I'd like to visit...	मैं...के लिए यात्रा करना चाहूंगा / चाहूंगी *main...ke liye yaatra karna chahoonga m /chahoongi f*
I'm late.	मैं देर से हूं। *main der se hoon*
Can you drive faster/slower?	क्या और तेज/धीमे चला सकते हैं? *kya aur tez/dheemain chala sakte hain?*
Stop/Wait here.	यहां रुकें/प्रतीक्षा करें। *yahan rukein/prateeksha karein*
How much?	कितना? *kitna?*
I'll pay ... rupee.	मैं...रुपये दूंगा। *main...rupee doonga*

You said it would cost...
आपने बताया था कि...की लागत इतनी पड़ेगी।
aapne bataya tha ki...ki lagat itni padegi

Keep the change.
खुले अपने पास रखो। *khule apne paas rakho*

YOU MAY HEAR...

कहां के लिए? *kahan ke liye?*
Where to?

पता क्या है? *pata kya hai?*
What's the address?

यह रात के समय/हवाई अड्डे का सरचार्ज है।
yah raat ke samaya/hawai adde ka surcharge hai
There's a nighttime/ airport surcharge.

Taxis and rickshaws are an easy and inexpensive means of getting around. Rickshaws can be tricycle-type contracptions with two seats on the back, or auto-rickshaws with motors, known simply as autos. Be prepared to haggle with the driver (**wallah**) on the fare however before you set off.

Bicycle, Motorbike & Rickshaw

I'd like to hire...	मैं किराये पर...चाहता / चाहती हूं।	
	*main kiraye par...chahta **m** / chahti **f** hoon*	
a bicycle	एक साइकिल *ek cycle*	
a moped	एक मोपेड *ek moped*	
a motorcycle	एक मोटरसाइकिल *ek motorcycle*	
a rickshaw	एक रिक्शा *ek rickshaw*	
a cycle-rickshaw	एक साइकिल रिक्शा *ek cycle-rickshaw*	
an auto rickshaw	एक ऑटो रिक्शा *ek auto rickshaw*	

How much per day/week?	कितना प्रति दिन/सप्ताह?
	kitna prati din/saptaah?
Can I have a helmet/lock?	क्या मुझे हेलमेट/ताला मिल सकता है?
	kya mujhe helmet/taala mil sakya hai?
I have a puncture/flat tyre.	मेरा टायर पंक्चर/बेकार हो गया है।
	mera tyre puncture/bekaar ho gaya hai

Car Hire

Where's the car hire?	किराये पर कार कहां मिलेगी?
	kiraaye par car kahan milegi?
I'd like...	मैं...पसंद करूंगा / करूंगी।
	main...pasand karoonga m / karoongi f
a cheap/small car	एक सस्ती/छोटी कार *ek sasti/choti car*
an automatic/a manual	एक स्वचालित/एक मैनुअल
	ek swachalit/ek manual
air conditioning	एयर कंडीशनिंग *air conditioning*
a car seat	एक कार सीट *ek car seat*
How much...?	कितना...? *kitna?*
per day/week	प्रति दिन/सप्ताह *prati din/saptaah*
per kilometer	प्रति किलोमीटर *prati kilometer*
for unlimited mileage	असीमित माइलेज के लिए *asimit mileage ke liye*

| with insurance | बीमा सहित *bema sahit* |
| Are there any discounts? | क्या कोई छूट है? *kya koi chhoot hai* |

YOU MAY HEAR...

क्या आपके पास अंतर्राष्ट्रीय ड्राइवर लाइसेंस है? *kya aapke paas antarrashtriya driver hai?*	Do you have an international driver's license?
कृपया, अपना पासपोर्ट दें। *kripya, apna paasport dein*	Your passport, please.
क्या आप बीमा चाहते हैं। *kya aap bema chahte hain?*	Do you want insurance?
मैं जमा चाहूंगा *main jama chahoonga*	I'll need a deposit.
यहां आद्यक्षर/हस्ताक्षर करें *prarambhik/yahan hastakshar karein*	Initial/Sign here.

Car & Driver

I'd like to hire a car with driver please.	कृपया मैं ड्राइवर सहित कार किराये पर चाहूंगा। *kripya main driver sahit car kiraye par chahoonga*
How much...?	कितना...? *kitna?*
per day/week	प्रति दिन/सप्ताह *prati din/saptaah*
to go to...	...के लिए जाने को *...ke liye jaane ko*
Is this your best price?	क्या यह आपका सर्वोत्तम मूल्य है? *kya yah aapka sarvottam mulya hai?*
What time are we leaving?	हम किस समय प्रस्थान कर रहे हैं? *hum kis samaya prasthan kar rahein hain?*
What time will we get there?	हम किस समय वहां पहुंचेंगे? *hum kis samaya wahan pahoonchenge?*
Can we stop here?	क्या हम यहां रुक सकते हैं? *kya hum yahan ruk sakte hain?*

Fuel Station

Where's the fuel station?	ईंधन स्टेशन कहां है? *eeindhan station kahan hai?*
Fill it up.	इसे भर दें। *ise bhar dein*
...rupee, please.	कृपया,...रुपये दें। *kripya, ...rupee dein*
I'll pay in cash/by credit card.	मैं नकद/क्रेडिट कार्ड से भुगतान करूंगा। *main nakad/credit card se bhugtaan karoonga*

For Numbers, see page 165.

YOU MAY SEE...

गैस [पेट्रोल]	gas [petrol]
लेड रहित	unleaded
नियमित	regular
सुपर	premium [super]
डीजल	diesel

Asking Directions

Is this the way to...?	क्या यह...को जाने का रास्ता है? *kya yah...ko jaane ka raasta hai?*
How far is it to...?	यह...से कितनी दूर है? *yah...se kitni door hai?*
Where's...?	...कहां है? *...kahan hai?*
...Street	...सड़क *...sadak*
this address	यह पता *yah pata*
the highway [motorway]	राजमार्ग [मोटरमार्ग] *raajmarg [motorway]*
Can you show me on the map?	क्या आप मुझे मानचित्र पर दिखा सकते हैं? *kya aap mujhe maanchitra par dikha sakte hain*
I'm lost.	मैं खो गया। *main kho gaya*

YOU MAY HEAR...

बिल्कुल सीधे *bilkul seedhe*	straight ahead
बाएं *baayein*	left
दाएं *daayein*	right
कोने के आसपास *kone ke aaspaas*	around the corner
सामने *saamne*	opposite
पीछे *peechhe*	behind
उसके बगल में *uske bagal main*	next to
बाद *baad*	after
उत्तर/दक्षिण *uttar/dakshin*	north/south
पूरब/ पश्चिम *purab/pashchim*	east/west
ट्रैफिक लाइट पर *traffic light par*	at the traffic light
चौराहे पर *chaurahe par*	at the intersection

Parking

Can I park here?	क्या मैं यहां पार्क कर सकता / सकती हूं?
	*kya main yahan park kar sakta **m** / sakti **f** hoon?*
Where's...?	...कहां है? *... kahan hai?*
the parking garage	पार्किंग गैराज *parking garage*
the parking lot [car park]	पार्किंग लॉट [कार पार्क] *parking lot [car park]*
the parking meter	पार्किंग मीटर *parking meter*
How much...?	कितना...? *kitna?*
per hour	प्रति घंटे *prati ghante*
per day	प्रति दिन *prati din*
for overnight	रातभर के लिए *raatbhar ke liye*

YOU MAY SEE...

STOP	**STOP**	stop
	मार्ग दें	yield
	नो पार्किंग	no parking
	एक ही रास्ता	one way
	प्रवेश नही	no entry
	वाहनों की अनुमति नहीं	no vehicles allowed
	नो पासिंग	no passing
	आगे ट्रैफिक सिग्नल	traffic signals ahead
	निकास	exit

Driving in India is not for the fainthearted. Roads can be congested and dangerous, and there are many unwritten rules that you will need to be aware of. A safer, and often cheaper option is to rent a car and driver, see page 32.

Breakdown & Repair

My car broke down /won't start.	मेरी कार खराब हो गई है/ चालू नहीं हो रही है। *meri car kharab ho gayi hai/ chalu nahin ho rahi hai*
Can you fix it (today)?	क्या आप इस...को (आज) ठीक कर सकते हैं? *kya aap is...ko (Aaj) thik kar sakte hain?*
When will it be ready?	यह कब तैयार हो जाएगी? *yah kab taiyaar ho jaayegi?*
How much?	कितना *kitna?*

Accidents

| There was an accident. | एक दुर्घटना हुई। *ek durghatna hui* |
| Call an ambulance/ the police. | एंबुलेंस/पुलिस को बुलाओ। *ambulance/police ko bulao* |

ESSENTIAL

Can you recommend a hotel?	क्या आप एक होटल सुझा सकते हैं? *kya aap ek hotel sujha sakte hain?*
I made a reservation.	मैंने आरक्षण कराया। *maine aarakshan karaya*
My name is...	मेरा नाम...है। *mera naam...hai*
Do you have a room...?	क्या आपके पास एक कमरा है...? *kya aapke paas ek kamra hai?*
for one/two	एक/दो के लिए *ek/do ke liye*
with a bathroom	बाथरूम सहित *bathroom sahit*
with air conditioning	एयर कंडीशनिंग सहित *air conditioning sahit*
For...	...के लिए *...ke liye*
tonight	आज रात *aaj raat*
two nights	दो रातों *do raaton*
one week	एक सप्ताह *ek saptaah*
How much?	कितना? *kitna?*
Is there anything cheaper?	क्या कोई सस्ती चीज है? *kya koi sasti cheez hai?*
When's checkout?	चेकआउट कब है? *checkout kab hai?*
Can I leave this in the safe?	क्या मैं सेफ में इसे छोड़ सकता / सकती हूं? *kya main safe main ise chhod sakta **m** / sakti **f** hoon?*
Can I leave my bags?	क्या मैं अपने बैगों को छोड़ सकता / सकती हूं? *kya main apne baigon ko chhod sakta **m** / sakti **f** hoon?*
Can I have my bill/ a receipt?	क्या मुझे मेरा बिल/रसीद मिल सकता है। *Kya mujhe mera bill/rasid mil sakta hai?*
I'll pay in cash/by credit card.	मैं नकद/क्रेडिट कार्ड से भुगतान करूंगा / करूंगी। *main nakad/credit card se bhugtaan karoonga **m** / karoongi **f***

Lodging options in India include budget guesthouses, mid-range hotels, national park safari lodges, and five star luxury and heritage hotels. Heritage homestays are the equivalent to boutique hotels / B&Bs. State-run tourist bungalows can be found in many areas but the standard, facilities and amenities vary greatly. Another budget option is Ddharamshalas (pilgrims' guesthouses) and gurudwaras (Sikh temples). They usually expect a small donation but some may charge a fixed nominal fee.

Somewhere to Stay

Can you recommend...?	क्या आप...सुझा सकते है? *kya aap...sujha sakte hain?*
a beach resort	एक बीच रिजॉर्ट *ek beach resort*
a hotel	एक होटल *ek hotel*
a hostel	एक हॉस्टल *ek hostel*
a national park	एक राष्ट्रीय उद्यान *ek rashtriya udyaan*
a tiger reserve	एक बाघ अभयारण्य *ek baagh abhayaaranya*
a safari lodge	एक सफारी लॉज *ek safari lodge*
a bed and breakfast (B&B)	एक बेड और ब्रेकफास्ट (बीएंडबी) *ek bed aur breakfast (B&B)*
What is it near?	उसके पास क्या है? *uske paas kya hai?*
How do I get there?	मैं वहां कैसे पहुंचू? *main wahan kaise pahoonchu?*

At the Hotel

I have a reservation.	मेरे पास एक आरक्षण है। *mere paas ek aarakshan hai*
My name is...	मेरा नाम ... है। *mera naam ... hai*
Do you have a room...?	क्या आपके पास...कमरा है? *kya aapke paas... kamra hai?*
with a toilet/shower	शौचालय/शॉवर सहित *shauchalaya/shower sahit*
with air conditioning	एयर कंडीशनिंग सहित

In India, tipping is not mandatory but it is expected for a service. Expect to pay the following:

Parking valet – Rs 20

Bell boy carrying luggage to room – Rs 50

Other service (getting medicines and such) – Rs 40

Laundry valet – Rs 40

Room service for snacks – Rs 40

Room service for large meals – Rs40-50

Housekeeping – Rs 50

Doorman – Rs 20

that's smoking/ non-smoking	वह स्मोकिंग/गैर-स्मोकिंग है	*vah smoking/ gair-smoking hai*
For...	...के लिए	*...ke liye*
tonight	आज रात	*aaj raat*
two nights	दो रातों	*do raaton*
a week	एक सप्ताह	*ek saptaah*
Do you have...?	क्या आपके पास...है?	*kya aapke paas...hai?*
a computer	एक कंप्यूटर	*ek computer*
an elevator [a lift]	एक एलीवेटर [एक लिफ्ट]	*ek elevator [ek lift]*
(wireless) internet service	[वायरलेस] इंटरनेट सेवा	*(wireless) internet sewa*
room service	रूम सेवा	*room sewa*
a pool	एक पूल	*ek pool*
a gym	एक जिम	*ek gym*
I need...	मुझे...की आवश्यकता है।	*mujhe...ki aavashyakta hai*
an extra bed	एक अतिरिक्त बेड	*ek atirikt bed*
a cot	एक खाट	*ek khat*
a crib	एक पालने की	*ek paalne ki*

For Numbers, see page 165.

YOU MAY HEAR...

कृपया पासपोर्ट/क्रेडिट कार्ड दें।
kripya, passport/credit card dein

यह फॉर्म भरें। *yah form bharein*

यहां हस्ताक्षर करें। *yahan hastaakshar karein*

Your passport/credit card, please.

Fill out this form.

Sign here.

Price

How much per night/week?	प्रति रात/सप्ताह कितना? *prati raat/saptaah kitna?*
Does that include breakfast/tax?	क्या उसमें ब्रेकफास्ट/कर शामिल हैं? *kya usmain breakfast/kar shamil hain?*
Are there any discounts?	क्या कोई छूट है? *kya loi chhoot hai?*

Preferences

Can I see the room?	क्या मैं कमरा देख सकता / सकती हूं? *kya main kamra dekh sakta **m** / sakti **f** hoon?*
I'd like a... room.	मैं एक...कमरा चाहता / चाहती हूं? *main ek...kamra chahta **m** / chahti **f** hoon*
better	बेहतर *behtar*
bigger	बड़ा *bada*
cheaper	सस्ता *sasta*
quieter	शांतिपूर्ण *shantipoorna*
I'll take it.	मैं इसे ले लूंगा / लूंगी *main ise le loonga **m** / loongi **f***
No, I won't take it.	मैं इसे नहीं लूंगा / लूंगी। *main ise nahin loonga **m** / loongi **f***

Questions

Where is/are…?	…कहां है/हैं? *kahan hai/hain?*
the bar	एक बार *ek bar*
the bathrooms	एक बाथरूम *ek bathroom*
the elevator [lift]	एलीवेटर *elevator [lift]*
I'd like…	मैं…चाहूंगा *main…chahoonga*
a blanket	एक कंबल *ek kambal*
an iron	एक इस्तरी *ek istari*
the room	एक कमरा *ek kamra*
key/key card	चाबी/चाबी कार्ड *chabi/chabi card*
a pillow	एक तकिया *ek takiya*
soap	साबुन *saabun*
toilet paper	टॉयलेट *isij* toilet paper
a towel	एक तौलिया *ek tauliya*
Do you have an adapter for this?	क्या इसके लिए आपके पास एक एडैप्टर है? *kya iske liye aapke paas ek adapter hai?*
How do you turn on the lights?	आप लाइट कैसे जलाएंगे? *aap light kaise jalaenge?*
Can you wake me at…?	क्या आप मुझे…बजे जगा सकते हैं? *kya aap mujhe…baje jaga sakte hain?*
Can I leave this in the safe?	क्या मैं इसे सेफ में छोड़ सकता / सकती हूं? *kya main ise safe main chhod sakta **m** / sakti **f** hoon?*

YOU MAY SEE...

धकेलें/खींचें	push/pull
बाथरूम [टॉयलेट]	bathroom [toilet]
शॉवर	showers
एलीवेटर [लिफ्ट]	elevator [lift]
सीढ़ियां	stairs
वेंडिंग मशीन	vending machines
बर्फ	ice
लॉन्ड्री	laundry
परेशान नहीं करा	do not disturb
अग्नि दरवाजा	fire door
(आपातकालीन) निकास	emergency/fire exit
जगाने की कॉल	wake-up call

Can I have my things from the safe?	क्या मैं सेफ से अपनी चीजें ले सकता / सकती हूं? *kya main safe se apni cheezen le sakta m / sakti f hoon?*
Is there mail /a message for me?	क्या मेरे लिए कोई मेल/मैसेज है? *kya mere liye koi mail/message hai?*
Do you have a laundry service?	क्या आपके पास लॉन्ड्री सेवा है? *kya aapke paas laundry sewa hai?*

Problems

There's a problem.	एक समस्या है। *ek samasya hai*
I lost my key/key card.	मैंने अपनी चाबी/चाबी कार्ड को खो दिया। *maine apni chabi/chabi card ko kho diya*
I've locked my key/ key card in the room.	मैंने अपनी चाबी/चाबी कार्ड को कमरे में बंद कर दिया है। *maine apni chabi/chabi card ko kamre main band kar diya hai*
There's no hot water/toilet paper.	गरम पानी/टॉयलेट पेपर नहीं हैं। *garam paani/toilet paper nahin hai*

The room is dirty.	कमरा गंदा है। *kamra ganda hai*
There are bugs in the room.	कमरे में खटमल हैं। *kamre main khatmal hain*
the air conditioning	एयर कंडीशनिंग *air conditioning*
the fan	पंखा *pankha*
the heat [heating]	हीट [हीटिंग] *heat [heating]*
the light	लाइट *light*
the TV	टीवी *TV*
the toilet	टॉयलेट *toilet*
. . .doesn't work.	. . .काम नहीं करता है। *. . .kaam nahin karta hai*
Can you fix. . .?	क्या आप...ठीक कर सकते हैं? *kya aap. . .thik kar sakte hain?*
I'd like another room.	मैं दूसरा कमरा चाहूंगा / चाहूंगी। *main doosra kamra chahoonga m / chahoongi f*

Unlike the U.S., most of India runs on 220-volt electricity, and sockets are usually of the two-round pin variety, but do vary. You may need a converter and/or an adapter for your appliance.

Checking Out

When's checkout?	चेकआउट कब है? *checkout kab hai?*
Can I leave my bags here until…?	क्या मैं…तक अपने बैगों को यहां छोड़ सकता / सकती हूं? *kya main…tak apne baigon ko yahan chhod sakta m / sakti f hoon?*
Can I have an itemized bill/ a receipt?	क्या मुझे विस्तृत बिल/रसीद मिल सकता/सकती है? *kya mjhe vistrit bill/rasid mil sakte/sakti hain/hai?*
I think there's a mistake.	मुझे लगता है कि एक गलती है। *mujhe lagta hai ki ek galati hai*
I'll pay in cash/by credit card.	मैं नकद/क्रेडिट कार्ड से भुगतान करूंगा / करूंगी। *main nakad/credit card se bhugtaan karoonga m / karoongi f*

Renting

I reserved an apartment/a room.	मैंने एक अपार्टमेंट/एक कमरा आरक्षित किया। *maine ek apartment/ek kamra aarakshit kiya*
My name is…	मेरा नाम…है। *mera naam…hai*
Can I have the keys?	क्या मुझे चाबियां मिल सकती हैं? *kya mujhe chabiyaan mil sakti hain?*
Are there…?	क्या…हैं? *kya…hain?*
dishes	डिश *dish*
pillows	तकिए *takiye*
sheets	शीट *sheet*
towels	तौलिए *tauliye*
kitchen utensils	बर्तन *bartan*
When do I put out the bins /recycling?	मैंने कब कूड़ेदान/रीसाइकिलिंग को बाहर रखा है? *maine kab koodeda/recycling ko bahar rakha hai?*
…is broken.	…टूट गया है। *…toot gaya hai*
How does…work?	…कैसे काम करता है? *…kaise kaam karta hai?*
the air conditioner	एयर कंडीशनर *air conditioner*
the dishwasher	डिशवॉशर *dishwasher*
the freezer	फ्रीजर *freezer*

the heater	हीटर *heater*
the microwave	माइक्रोवेव *microwave*
the refrigerator	रेफिजरेटर *refrigerator*
the stove	स्टोव *stove*
the washing machine	वॉशिंग मशीन *washing machine*

For In the Kitchen, see page 81.

Domestic Items

I need...	मुझे...की आवश्यकता है। *mujhe. . . ki aavashyakta hai*
an adapter	एक एडैप्टर *ek adapter*
aluminum foil	एल्युमीनियम फॉयल *aluminium foil*
a basin/ bath plug	एक बेसिन/बाथ प्लग *ek basin/bath plug*
a bottle opener	एक बोतल ओपनर *ek bottle opener*
a broom	एक झाड़ू *ek jhaadu*
a can opener	एक कैन ओपनर *ek can opener*
cleaning supplies	क्लीनिंग आपूर्ति *cleaning aapurti*
a corkscrew	कॉर्कस्क्रू *corkscrew*
detergent	डिटर्जेंट *detergent*
dishwashing liquid	डिशवॉशिंग लिक्विड *dishwashing liquid*
bin bags	बिन बैग्स *bin bags*

a lightbulb	एक लाइटबल्ब	*ek light bulb*
matches	माचिस	*matches*
a mop	एक कूंचा	*ek kooncha*
mosquito net	मच्छरदानी	*machchardaani*
mosquito repellant	मच्छररोधी	*machcharrodhi*
napkins	नैप्किन	*napkin*
paper towels	पेपर तौलिए	*paper tauliye*
plastic wrap [cling film]	प्लास्टिक रैप [क्लिंग फिल्म]	*plastic wrap [cling film]*
a plunger	एक प्लंजर	*ek plunger*
scissors	कैंची	*kainchi*
a vacuum cleaner	एक वैक्यूम क्लीनर	*ek vaccum cleaner*

For Oven temperatures, see page 172.

At the Hostel

Is there a bed available?	क्या कोई बिस्तर उपलब्ध है?	*kya koi bistar uplabdh hai?*
I'd like...	मैं...पसंद करूंगा / करूंगी।	*main...pasand karoonga m /karoongi f*
a single/double room	एक सिंगल/डबल कमरा	*ek single/double kamra*
a blanket	एक कंबल	*ek kambal*
a pillow	एक तकिया	*ek takiya*
sheets	शीट	*sheet*
a towel	एक तौलिया	*ek tauliya*
What is the charge per day/week?	प्रति दिन/सप्ताह का किराया क्या है?	*prati din/saptaah ka kiraya kya hai?*
Do you have lockers?	क्या आपके पास लॉकर हैं?	*kya aapke paas locker hai?*
Are there...?	क्या कोई...हैं?	*kya koi...hain?*
cooking facilities	कुकिंग सुविधाएं	*cooking suvidhayein*
electric outlets	इलेक्ट्रिक आउटलेट	*electric outlet*

पेय जल
DRINKING WATER

←

laundry facilities	लॉन्ड्री सुविधाएं	*laundry suvidhayein*
showers	शॉवर	*shower*
When do you lock up?	आपने कब बंद किया?	*aapne kab band kiya?*
Do I need a membership card?	मुझे सदस्यता कार्ड की आवश्यकता है।	*mujhe sadasyata card ki aavashyakta hai?*
Here's my international student card.	यह मेरा अंतर्राष्ट्रीय छात्र कार्ड है।	*yah mera antarrashtriya kshatra card hai*

For Domestic Items, see page 45.

YOU MAY SEE...

पेय जल	drinking water
पड़ाव निषेध	no camping
अग्नि/बार्बेक्यू नहीं	no fires/barbecues

Communications

ESSENTIAL

Where's an internet cafe?	इंटरनेट कैफे कहां है? *internet cafe kahan hai?*
Can I access the internet/check my email?	क्या मैं इंटरनेट पहुंच हासिल कर/अपनी ईमेल देख सकता / सकती हूं? *kya main internet pahunch haasil kar/apni email dekh sakta m / sakti f hoon?*
How much per hour/hour?	प्रति आधा घंटा/घंटा कितना? *prati aadha ghanta/ghanta kitna?*
How do I connect/log on?	मैं कैसे कनेक्ट/लॉग ऑन कर सकता / सकती हूं? *main kaise connect/log on kar sakta m / sakti f hoon?*
A phone card, please.	कृपया, फोन कार्ड दें। *kripya, phone card dein*
Can I have your phone number?	क्या मुझे आपका फोन नंबर मिल सकता हैं? *kya mujhe aapka phone number mil sakta hai?*
Here's my number/email.	यह मेरा नंबर/ईमेल है। *yah mera number/email hai*
Call me.	मुझे कॉल करें। *mujhe call karein*
Email me.	मुझे ईमेल करें। *mujhe email karein*
Hello. This is...	हैलो। यह...है। *hello. yah...hai*
Can I speak to...?	क्या मैं...से बात कर सकता / सकती हूं? *kya main...se baat kar sakta m / sakti f hoon?*
Can you repeat that?	क्या आप उसे दोहरा सकते हैं? *kya aap use dohra sakte hain?*
I'll call back later.	मैं बाद में कॉल करूंगा / करूंगी। *main baad main call karoonga m / karoongi f*
Bye.	अलविदा *alvida*
Where's the post office?	डाक घर कहां है? *daak ghar kahan hai?*
I'd like to send this to...	मैं इसे...को भेजना चाहता / चाहती हूं। *main ise...ko bhejna chahta m / chahti f hoon*

Internet access is widely available, either in guesthouses and
hotels or in dedicated cybercafés. Away from the big cities,
connections can be slow and unreliable, with antiquated dial-up
connections and frustrating service interruptions.

Online

Where's an internet cafe?	इंटरनेट कैफे कहां है? *internet cafe kahan hai?*
Does it have wireless internet?	क्या इसके पास वायरलेस इंटरनेट है? *kya aapke paas wireless internet hai?*
What is the WiFi password?	वाईफाई पासवर्ड क्या है? *wifi password kya hai?*
Is the WiFi free?	क्या वाईफाई मुफ़्त है? *kya wifi muft hai?*
Do you have bluetooth?	क्या आपके पास ब्लूटूथ है? *kya aapke paas Bluetooth hai?*
Can you show me how to turn on/ off the computer?	क्या आप दिखा सकते हैं कि कंप्यूटर को कैसे खोलना/ बंद करना है? *kya aap dikha sakte hain ki computer ko kaise kholna/ band karna hai?*
Can I...?	क्या मैं...सकता / सकती हूं? *kya main...sakta **m** / sakti **f** hoon?*

access the internet	इंटरनेट पहुंच	*internet pahoonch*
check my email	अपनी ईमेल देख	*apni email dekh*
print	प्रिंट कर	*print kar*
plug in/charge my laptop/iPhone/iPad /BlackBerry?	अपना लैपटॉप चार्ज/आईफोन/आईपैड/ब्लैकबेरी प्लग इन/चार्ज कर	*apna laptop /iphone/ipad/blackberry plug in/charge kar*
access Skype?	स्काइप पहुंच	*skype pahoonch hai?*
How much per half hour/hour?	प्रति आधा घंटा/घंटा कितना?	*prati aadha ghanta/ghante kitna?*
How do I . . . ?	मैं...कैसे करूं?	*main . . . kaise karoon?*
connect/disconnect	कनेक्ट/डिस्कनेक्ट	*connect/disconnect*
log on/off	लॉग ऑन/ऑफ	*log on/off*
type this symbol	इस प्रतीक को टाइप करो	*is prateek ko type karo*
What's your email?	आपका ईमेल क्या है?	*aapka email kya hai?*
My email is . . .	मेरा ईमेल...है।	*mera email. . .hai*
Do you have a scanner?	क्या आपके पास स्कैनर है?	*kya aapke paas scanner hai?*

Social Media

Are you on Facebook/Twitter?	क्या आप फेसबुक/ट्विटर पर हैं?	*kya aap facebook/twitter par hain?*
What's your username?	आपका यूजरनेम क्या है?	*aapka username kya hai?*
I'll add you as a friend.	मैं आपको मित्र के रूप में जोड़ूंगा / जोड़ूंगी।	*main aapko mitra ke roop main jodoonga **m** / jodoongi **f***
I'll follow you on Twitter.	मैं आपको ट्विटर पर फॉलो करूंगा / करूंगी।	*main aapko twitter par follow karoonga **m** / aroongi **f***
Are you following . . . ?	क्या आप...फॉलो कर रहे हैं?	*kya aap. . . follow kar rahe hain?*
I'll put the pictures on Facebook/Twitter.	मैं फेसबुक/ट्विटर पर तस्वीरें रखूंगा / रखूंगी।	*main facebook/twitter par tasveerein rakhoonga **m** / rakhoongi **f***
I'll tag you in the pictures.	मैं आपको तस्वीरों में टैग करूंगा /करूंगी।	*main aapko tasveeron main tag karoonga **m** / karoongi **f***

YOU MAY SEE…

बंद	close
हटाएं	delete
ईमेल	email
निकास	exit
सहायता	help
इंस्टेंट मेसेंजर	instant messenger
इंटरनेट	internet
लॉग	log in
नया (संदेश)	new (message)
ऑन/ऑफ	on/off
खोलें	open
प्रिंट करें	print
सहेजें	save
भेजें	send
यूजरनेम/पासवर्ड	username/password
वायरलेस इंटरनेट	wireless internet

Phone

A phone card/prepaid phone, please.	कृपया, फोन कार्ड/प्रीपेड फोन दें। *kripya, phone card/prepaid phone dein*
How much?	कितना? *kitna?*
Where's the pay phone?	पे फोन कहां है? *pay phone kahan hai?*
What's the area country code for…?	…के लिए एरिया कंट्री कोड क्या है? *. . . ke liye area country code kya hai?*
What's the number for Information?	सूचना के लिए नंबर क्या है? *soochna ke liye number kya hai?*
I'd like the number for…	मुझे…के लिए नंबर चाहिए होगा। *mujhe. . . ke liye number chahiye hoga*
I'd like to call collect [reverse the charges].	मैं कॉल कलेक्ट [प्रभारों को विपरित] करना चाहूंगा/चाहूंगी। *main call collect [prabharon ko viprit] karna chahoonga/chahoongi*
My phone doesn't work here.	मेरा फोन यहां काम नहीं करता है। *mera phone yahan kaam nahin karta hai*
What network are you on?	आप किस नेटवर्क पर हैं? *aap kis network par hain*
Is it 3G?	क्या यह ३जी है? *kya yah 3G hai?*
I have run out of credit/minutes.	मेरे पास क्रेडिट/मिनट कम पड़ गए हैं। *mere paas credit/minute kam pad gaye hain*

Can I buy some credit? क्या मैं कुछ क्रेडिट ख़रीद सकता / सकती हूं?
kya main kuch credit kharid sakta m / sakti f hoon?

Do you have a phone charger? क्या आपके पास फोन चार्जर है?
kya aapke paas phone charger hai?

Can I have your number? क्या मुझे आपका नंबर मिल सकता है?
kya mujhe aapka number mil sakta hai?

Here's my number. यह मेरा नंबर है। *yah mera number hai*

Please call/text me. कृपया मुझे कॉल/टेक्स्ट करें।
kripya, mujhe call/text karein

I'll call/text you. मैं आपको कॉल/टेक्स्ट करूंगा / करूंगी।
main aapko call/text karoonga m / karoongi f

For Numbers, see page 165.

YOU MAY HEAR...

कौन कॉल कर रहा है? *kaun call kar raha hai?* — Who's calling?

रोक कर रखें। *rok kar rakhein* — Hold on.

मैं आपको उनसे मिला दूंगा / दूंगी।
main aapko unse mila doonga m / doongi f — I'll put you through.

वह यहां नहीं/दूसरी लाइन पर है ।
vah yahan nahin/doosri line par hai — He/She is not here/on another line.

क्या आप कोई संदेश छोड़ना चाहते हैं?
kya aap koi sandesh chhodna chahte hain? — Would you like to leave a message?

बाद में/दस मिनट में वापस कॉल करें।
baad main/das minute main wapas call karein — Call back later/in ten minutes.

क्या वह आपको वापस कॉल कर सकता / सकती है। Can he/she call you back?
kya vah aapko wapas call kar sakta m / sakti hai f

आपका नंबर क्या है? *aapka number kya hai?* — What's your number?

Telephone Etiquette

Hello. This is...	हेलो/नमस्ते। यह...है।	*hello. Yah...hai*
Can I speak to...?	क्या मैं....से बात कर सकता / सकती हूं?	
		*kya main...se baat kar sakta **m** / sakti **f** hoon?*
Extension...	विस्तार...	*vistaar*
Speak louder/more slowly, please.	कृपया, तेज/थोड़ा धीमे बोलें।	
		ripya, tez/thoda dheemein bolein
Can you repeat that?	क्या आप उसे दोहरा सकते हैं?	
		kya aap use dohra sakte hain?

Indian telephone numbers are all 10 digits long (including the area code, minus the initial 0). Mobile phone numbers are also 10 digits. Privately run telephone services with international facilities are widespread and can be recognised by the acronyms STD/ISD (standard trunk dialling/ international subscriber dialing). Home country direct services are available from any telephone to most countries. These allow you to make reverse charges or telephone credit card calls abroad via the operator in that country.

YOU MAY HEAR...

सीमा शुल्क घोषणा फॉर्म भरें।
sima shulk form bharein

कीमत क्या है? *keemat kya hai?*

इसके अंदर क्या है?
iske ander kya hai?

Fill out the customs
declaration form.

What's the value?

What's inside?

I'll call back later.	मैं आपको बाद में कॉल करता / करती हूं। *main aapko baad mein call karta **m** / karti **f** hoon*
Bye.	अलविदा *alvida*

Fax

Can I send/receive a fax here?	क्या मैं यहां फैक्स भेज/प्राप्त कर सकता / सकती हूं? *kya main yahan fax bhej/prapt kar sakta **m** / sakti **f** hoon?*
What's the fax number?	फैक्स नंबर क्या है? *fax number kya hai?*
Please fax this to...	कृपया इसे...के लिए फैक्स करें। *kripya, ise...ke liye fax karein*

Post

Where's the post office/mailbox?	डाक घर/मेलबॉक्स कहां है। *daak ghar/mailbox kahan hai?*
A stamp for this postcard/letter to...	...के लिए यह पोस्टकार्ड/चिट्ठी हेतु एक डाक टिकट *...ke liye yak postcard/chitthi hetu ek dak ticket*
How much?	कितना? *kitna?*
Send this package by airmail/express.	इस पैकेज को एयरमेल/एक्सप्रेस से भेज दें। *is package ko airmail/express se bhej dein*
A receipt, please.	कृपया, रसीद दें। *kripya, rasid dein.*

Food & Drink

Eating Out

ESSENTIAL

Can you recommend a good restaurant/bar?	क्या आप मुझे एक अच्छा रेस्तरां/बार सुझा सकते हैं? *kya aap mujhe ek achcha restaurant/bar sujha sakte hain*
Is there a traditional/ an inexpensive restaurant nearby?	क्या यहां पास में कोई पारंपरिक/सस्ता रेस्तरां है? *kya yahan paas main koi paramparik/sasta restaurant hai?*
A table for..., please.	कृपया,...के लिए मेज *kripya...ke liye mez*
Can we sit...?	क्या हम...बैठ सकते हैं? *kya hum...baith sakte hain?*
here/there	यहां/वहां *yahan/wahan*
outside	बाहर *bahar*
in a non-smoking area	धूम्रपान- निषेध क्षेत्र में *dhoomrapaan nishedh kshetra main*
I'm waiting for someone.	मैं किसी की प्रतीक्षा कर रहा हूं! *main kisi ki pratiksha kar raha hoon*
Where are the toilets?	शौचालय कहां हैं? *shauchalaya kahan hai?*
The menu, please.	कृपया, मेनू दें! *kripya menu dein*
What do you recommend?	आप क्या सुझाव देते हैं? *aap kya sujhav de sakte hain?*
I'd like...	मैं...चाहूंगा! *main...chahoonga*
Some more..., please.	कृपया...कुछ और! *kripya kuch aur*
Enjoy your meal!	अपने भोजन का मजा लें! *apne bhojan ka maza lein*
The check [bill], please.	कृपया [बिल] जांच लें! *kripya [bill]jaanch lain*
Is service included?	क्या सेवा शामिल है? *kya seva shamil hai?*
Can I pay by credit card/have a receipt?	क्या मैं क्रेडिट कार्ड से भुगतान कर सकता हूं/क्या मुझे रसीद मिल सकती है? *kya main credit card se bhugtan kar sakta hoon/kya mujhe rasid mil sakti hai*

India offers a wide arrary of eateries, from street stalls to swanky restaurants. **Thalis** in the North or meals in the South generally include a variety of dishes and are often replenished free of charge. **Dhaba** or roadside restaurants offer great value as well as a great culinary experience. The most basic and traditional will double as truck stops, and often only have **charpoi**, a wooden framed bed with a latticed cloth top to sit on. More sophisticated examples will feature tables and chairs and menu cards in English.

Where to Eat

Can you recommend...?	क्या आप...का सुझाव दे सकते हैं?
	kya aap. . . ka sujhav de sakte hain?
a restaurant	एक रेस्तरां *ek restaurant*
an authentic/ a non-touristy restaurant	एक विश्वसनीय/गैर-पर्यटन रेस्तरां
	ek vishwasniya/gair-paryatan restaurant

Reservations & Preferences

I'd like to reserve	मैं आरक्षित करना चाहूंगा
	main aarakshit karna chahoonga
a table...	...एक मेज ... *ek mez*
for two	दो के लिए *do ke liye*
for this evening	इस शाम के लिए *is sham ke liye*
a bar	एक बार *ek bar*
a café	एक कैफे *ek cafe*
a fast food place	एक फास्ट फूड प्लेस *ek fast food place*
a cheap restaurant	एक सस्ते रेस्तरां *ek saste restaurant*
an expensive restaurant	एक महंगे रेस्तरां *ek mahnge restaurant*
a restaurant with a good view	अच्छे दृश्य वाले एक रेस्तरां *achche drishya wale ek restaurant*
for tomorrow at...	कल के लिए...बजे। *kal ke liye...baje*
A table for two, please.	कृपया, दो के लिए मेज। *kripya, do ke liye mez*
I have a reservation.	मेरा आरक्षण है। *mera aarakshan hai*
My name is...	मेरा नाम...है। *mera naam...hai*
Can we sit...?	क्या हम...बैठ सकते हैं? *kya hum... baith sakte hain?*
here/there	यहां/वहां *yahan/wahan*
outside	बाहर *bahar*

YOU MAY HEAR...

क्या आपका आरक्षण है? *kya aapka aarakshan hai?*	Do you have a reservation?
कितने? *kitne*	How many?
धूम्रपान या गैर-धूम्रपान? *dhoomrapaan ya gair-dhoomrapaan?*	Smoking or non-smoking?
क्या आप (ऑर्डर के लिए) तैयार हैं? *kya aap (order ke liye) taiyaar hain?*	Are you ready (to order)?
आप क्या पसंद करेंगे? *aap kya pasand karenge?*	What would you like?
मैं...का सुझाव देता हूं! *main...ka sujhav deta hoon*	I recommend...
अपने भोजन का मजा लें *apne bhojan ka maza lein*	Enjoy your meal.

in a non-smoking area	धूम्रपान निषेध क्षेत्र में	*dhoomrapaan nishedh ksetra main*
by the window	खिड़की के बगल में	*khidki ke bagal main*
in the shade	छांव में	*chaav main*
in the sun	धूप में	*dhoop main*
Where are the toilets?	शौचालय कहां हैं?	*shauchalaya kahan hai?*

How to Order

Excuse me, sir/ma'am?	माफ करिए, सर/मैडम?	*mujhe kshma kijiye, sir/madam?*
We're ready (to order).	हम तैयार हैं (ऑर्डर के लिए)	*hum taiyaar hain (order ke liye)*
The wine list, please.	कृपया, शराब की सूची दें।	*kripya, sharab ki suchi dein*
I'd like...	मैं...पंसद करूंगा	*main...pasand karoonga*
a bottle of...	...की एक बोतल	*....ki ek bottle*
a carafe of...	...की एक मीना	*...ki ek mina*
a glass of...	...का एक ग्लास	*...kaa ek glass*
The menu, please.	कृपया, मेनू दें।	*kripya, menu dein*
Do you have...?	क्या आपके पास...है?	*kya aapke paas...hai?*
a menu in English	अंग्रेजी में एक मेनू	*angrezi main ek menu*
a fixed price menu	नियत मूल्य मेनू	*niyat mulya menu*
a children's menu	बच्चों का मेनू	*bachchon ka menu*
What do you recommend?	आप क्या सुझाव देते हैं?	*aap kya sujhav dete hain?*
What's this?	यह क्या है?	*yah kya hai?*
What's in it?	इसमें क्या है?	*ismein kya hai?*

YOU MAY SEE...

कवर प्रभार	cover charge
नियत मूल्य	fixed price
मेनू (दिन का)	menu (of the day)
सेवा षामिल (नहीं)	service (not) included
विशेष	specials

Is it spicy?	क्या यह मसालेदार है? *kya yah masaledar hai?*
Without…, please.	कृपया,…के बगैरा *kripya,…ke bagair*
It's to go [take away].	यह ले जाने के लिए है [ले जाएं]। *yah le jaane liye hai [le jayein]*

Cooking Methods

baked	सिका हुआ *sikaa hua*
barbecued	सीक पर भुना *seenk pur bhunaa*
boiled	उबला *ublaa*
braised	दम किया हुआ *dum kiya hua*
breaded	ब्रेड किया हुआ *bread kiya hua*
creamed	क्रीम किया हुआ *cream kiya hua*
deep-fried	अधिक तेल में तला *adhik tel mein tala*

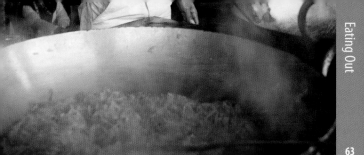

diced	टुकड़े किया हुआ	*tukade kya hua*
dry-fried	ड्राय-फ्रायड	*dry-fried*
filleted	फिलेट किया हुआ	*fillet kiya hua*
fried	तला हुआ	*tala hua*
grilled	ग्रिल किया हुआ	*grill kiya hua*
poached	पोच किया हुआ	*poach kiya hua*
roasted	सिंका हुआ	*sinka hua*
sautéed	सॉट किया हुआ	*saut kiya hua*
smoked	स्मोक किया हुआ	*smoke kiya hua*
steamed	भाप से पका	*bhaap se paka*
stewed	धीरे-धीरे उबालना	*dheere dheere*
stuffed	स्टफ किया हुआ	*stuff kiya hua*

Dietary Requirements

I'm...	मैं...हूं	*main...hoon*
diabetic	मधुमेह पीड़ित	*madhumeh pidit*
lactose intolerant	लैक्टोज के प्रति असहनशील	
	lactose ke prati asahanshil	
vegetarian	शाकाहारी	*shaakahari*
vegan	शुद्ध शाकाहारी	*shudh shakahaari*
I'm allergic to...	मुझे...से एलर्जी है।	*mujhe...se allergy hai*

I can't eat…	मैं…को नहीं खा सकता हूं। *main…ko nahin kha sakta hoon*
dairy products	डेयरी उत्पादों *dairy utpaadon*
gluten	ग्लूटेन *gluten*
nuts	मेवे *meve*
pork	सुअर मांस *suar maans*
shellfish	घोंघा *ghongha*
spicy foods	मसालेदार खाने *masaledaar khane*
wheat	गेहूं *gehoon*
Is it halal/kosher?	क्या यह हलाल/स्वच्छ है? *kyaa yah halal/swachchha hai?*
Do you have…?	क्या आपके पास…है? *kya aapke paas…hai?*
skimmed म्पसा	रिकम्ड दूध *skimmed doodh*
whole milk	पूरा दूध *poora doodh*
soya milk	सोया दूध *soya doodh*

Dining with Children

Do you have children's portions?	क्या आपके पास बच्चों के हिस्से हैं? *kya aapke paas bachchon ke hisse hain?*
A highchair/child's seat, please.	कृपया, ऊंची कुर्सी/बच्चे की सीट दें। *kripya, unchi kursi/bachche ki seat dain*

Where can I feed/ change the baby?	मैं कहां बच्चे को खिला/कपड़े बदलवा सकता / सकती हूं!
	*main kahan bachche ko khila/kapde badalwa sakta **m** / sakti **f** hoon?*
Can you warm this?	क्या आप इसे गर्म कर सकते हैं?
	kya aap ise garm kar sakte hain

For Traveling with Children, see page 143.

How to Complain

When will our food be ready?	हमारा भोजन कब तैयार होगा?
	hamara bhojan kab taiyaar hoga?
We can't wait any longer.	हम और प्रतीक्षा नहीं कर सकते हैं?
	hum aur prtiksha nahin kar sakte hain
We're leaving.	हम जा रहे हैं! *hum jaa rahe hain*
I didn't order this.	मैंने इसका ऑर्डर नहीं दिया! *maine iska order nahin diya hai*
I ordered...	मैंने...का ऑर्डर दिया! *maine...ka order diya*
I can't eat this.	मैं यह नहीं खा सकता हूं! *main yah nahin kha sakta hoon*
This is too...	यह बहुत... *yah bahut...*
cold/hot	ठंडा/गरम *thanda/garam*
salty/spicy	नमकीन/तीखा *namkeen/teekha*
tough/bland	कड़ा/नरम *kada/naram*
This isn't clean/fresh.	यह साफ/ताजा नहीं है! *yah saaf/taza nahin hai*

Paying

The check [bill], please.	कृपया, चेक। *kripya, check*
Separate checks [bills], please.	कृपया, अलग-अलग चेक *kripya, alag-alag check*
It's all together.	यह सब मिलाकर है। *yah sab milakar hai*
Is service included?	क्या सेवा शामिल है? *kya seva shamil hai?*
What's this amount for?	यह राशि किसके लिए है? *yah rashi kiske liye hai?*
I didn't have that.	मैंने वह नहीं खाया। *maine wah nahin khaya*
I had . . .	मैंने...खाया। *maine. . .khaya*
Can I have a receipt/ an itemized bill?	क्या मुझे रसीद/विस्तृत बिल मिल सकता है? *kya mujhe rasid/vistrit bill mil sakta hai?*
That was delicious!	यह बहुत स्वादिष्ट था! *Yah bahut swadishta tha*
I've already paid.	मैंने पहले ही भुगतान कर दिया है। *miane pahle hi bhugtaan kar diya hai*

For tipping, expect to pay the following: at a restaurant – 10 to 15% of the bill, either written into your credit card slip or as cash slipped into the folder. Fine dining restaurant – 15 to 20% of the bill. Maitre d' (for selecting wine or preparing a special meal) – Rs 100. Coffee shop – 10% of the bill.

Meals & Cooking

Breakfast

bacon	सूअर का मांस *suar ka maans*
bread	ब्रेड *bread*
butter	मक्खन *makhan*
coffee/tea...	कॉफी/चाय... *coffee/chay*
black	काली *kaali*
decaf	डीकैफ *decaf*
with milk	दूध के साथ *doodh ke saath*
with sugar	चीनी के साथ *chini ke saath*
with artificial sweetener	कृत्रिम स्वीटनर के साथ *kritim sweetner ke saath*
cold/hot cereal	ठंडा/गरम अनाज *thanda/garam anaaj*
cold cuts	सैंडविच मांस *sandwich maans*
croissant	क्रोइसैन *croissant*
jam/jelly	जैम/जेली *jam/jelly*
marmalade	मुरब्बा *murabba*
cheese	पनीर *paneer*
...juice	...जूस *juice*
Orange	संतरा *santra*
Apple	सेब *seb*
Grapefruit	चकोतरा *chakotra*
milk	दूध *doodh*
oatmeal [porridge]	जई दलिया [दलिया] *jai daliya*
granola [muesli]	ग्रेनोला [म्यूसली] *granola [muesli]*
muffin	टिकिया *tikiya*
...egg	...अंडा *anda*
Hard /Soft boiled	सख्त/नरम उबला हुआ *sakhta/naram ubla hua*
Fried	तला हुआ *tala hua*

Scrambled	तले *tale*
omelet	ऑमलेट *omelet*
toast	टोस्ट *toast*
roll	रोल *roll*
sausage	सॉस *sausage*
water	पानी *paani*
yogurt	दही *dahi*

Appetizers

राज कचौड़ी *raj kachori*	deep fried wheat pastry filled with potato, chick peas, and spices
दही भल्ला *dahi bhalla*	pastries made from lentils, served with yogurt and chutneys
गोल गप्पा *gol guppa*	fried puffs of dough filled with vegetables and spicy sauce
भेल पूरी *bhel puri*	puffed rice mixed with different vegetables and sauces
चाट *chaat*	yogurt and potatoes with sauces

छोले भटूरे *choley bhature* — seasoned garbanzo beans served with fresh fried bread

आलू की टिक्की *aloo ki tikki* — stuffed mashed potato cakes

ब्रेड पकौड़ा *bread pakora* — bread slices dipped in spicy chick pea flour batter and deep fried

ढोकला *dokhla* — steamed cubes of ground rice lentils, seasoned with mustard seeds and red chili

समोसा *samosa* — stuffed triangle-shaped pastries filled with mildly spiced potatoes

बर्गर *burger* — burger

ऑमलेट *omelette* — omelette

सैंडविच *sandwich* — sandwich

आम *aam* — mango

फ़ॅंच फ़्राइज *french fries* — french fries [chips]

हैमबर्गर *hamburger* — hamburger

कुकीज [बिस्कुट] *cookies [biscuit]* — cookies [biscuits]

केक *cake* — cake

सैंडविच *sandwich* — sandwich

आलू चिप्स [कुरकुरा]
aaloo chips [kurkuraa]

मूंगफली *moongphali*

चॉकलेट *chocolate*

हॉट डॉग *hot dog*

छोले भटूरे *choley bhature*

ब्रेड पकौड़ा *bread pakoda*

पनीर पकौड़ा *paneer pakoda*

समोसा *samosa*

potato chips [crisps]

peanuts

chocolate

hot dog

seasoned garbanzo beans
(choley) served with fresh
fried bread

bread slices dipped in spicy
chick pea flour batter and
deep fried

bread slices stuffed with
cheese dipped in spicy chick
pea flour batter and deep
fried.

stuffed triangle-shaped
pastries filled with mildly
spiced potatoes

Soup

टमाटर का सूप *tamater kaa soup*	tomato soup
वेज हॉट एंड सॉर सूप *veg hot and sour soup*	veg. hot & sour soup
वेज स्वीट कॉर्न सूप *veg sweet corn soup*	veg. sweet corn soup
चिकन सूप *chicken soup*	chicken soup
चिकन हॉट एंड सॉर सूप *chicken hot and sour soup*	chicken hot & sour soup
चिकन स्वीट कॉर्न सूप *chicken sweet corn soup*	chicken sweet corn soup
मशरूम सूप *mushroom soup*	mushroom soup
सब्जी का सूप *subjee kaa soup*	vegetable soup
टमाटर और तुलसी *tamater aur tulsi*	tomato & basil soup
चिकन पालक *chicken paalak*	chicken spinach soup
सब्जी तालू मियन *subjee taalu miyan*	vegetable talu mein

Fish & Seafood

ग्रास कार्प *grass carp*	grass carp
कैट फिश *catfish*	catfish
समुद्री बैस *samudri baas*	sea bass
हेरिंग *herring*	herring
सोल *sole*	sole
शार्क का पंख *shark ka pankh*	shark's fin
लाल स्नैपर *lal snapper*	red snapper

टुना *tuna* | tuna
कौड *cod* | cod
व्हाईट बैट *whitebait* | whitebait
ओएस्टर *oyster* | oysters
क्लैम्स *clamps* | clams
एबलोन *abalone* | abalone
स्कालोप्स *scallops* | scallops
बेबी स्किवड *baby squid* | baby squid
श्रिम्प *shrimp* | shrimp
बड़ा श्रिम्प *bada shrimp* | large shrimp
झींगा *jheenga* | lobster
मुसेल्स *mussels* | mussels
ट्राउट *trout* | trout

Meat & Poultry

गो मांस *go maans* | beef
मेमना/लैंब *memnaa/lamb* | lamb
सुअर का मांस/पोर्क *soour ka maans/pork* | pork
सुअर का सुखाया मांस/हैम | ham
soour ka sukhaya maans/ ham
सुअर का नमकीन मांस/बेकन | bacon
soour ka sukhaya maans/ bacon

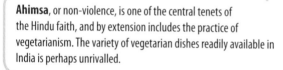

Ahimsa, or non-violence, is one of the central tenets of the Hindu faith, and by extension includes the practice of vegetarianism. The variety of vegetarian dishes readily available in India is perhaps unrivalled.

बछड़े का मांस/वील *bachde ka maans/veal*	veal
बकरा *bakra*	goat
स्प्रिंग कबूतर *spring kabootar*	spring pigeon
स्टीक *steak*	steak
कलेजी *kalejee*	liver
गुर्दा *gurda*	kidneys
सॉसेज *sausage*	sausages
बत्तख *batakh*	duck
टर्की *turkey*	turkey
चिकन *chicken*	chicken
हंस *huns*	goose
भुना या ग्रिल्ड चिकन *bhunee ya grilled*	roast or grilled chicken
मीठा और खट्टा *meetha aur khutta*	sweet and sour chicken
चिकन कलेजी *chicken kalejee*	liver

| भुनी बत्तख *bhuni batakh* | roast duck |
| पाइनेपल बत्तख *pineapple batakh* | pineapple duck |

Vegetables & Staples

बंदगोभी *bundhgobi*	cabbage
प्याज *pyaaz*	onion
मटर *mutter*	peas
हरे सेम *hare sem*	green beans
बैंगन *baingun*	eggplant [aubergine]
सलाद *salad*	lettuce
आलू *aaloo*	potatoes
मीठी लाल मिर्च *meethee lal mirch*	sweet red peppers
कुकुरमुत्ता *kukurmutta*	mushrooms
गाजर *gajar*	carrots
पालक *paalak*	spinach
अंकुरित सेम *ankurit sem*	bean sprouts
अंकुरित मटर *ankurit mutter*	pea sprouts
फूलगोभी *phoolgobi*	broccoli
अजवाइन *ajwain*	celery
खीरा *kheera*	cucumber
टमाटर *tamater*	tomato
शतावरी *shatawari*	asparagus

बैंबू शूट्स *bamboo shoots* — bamboo shoots
जलकुंभी *julkumbhi* — watercress
मटर *mutter* — snow peas [mangetout]
चावल *chawal* — rice
चावल दलिया *chawal daleeyaa* — rice porridge
सेम *sem* — beans

Bread

ब्रेड *bread* — bread
आलू परांठा *aaloo parantha* — flatbread stuffed with mashed potato
सादा परांठा *saada parantha* — flatbread
दाल परांठा *dal parantha* — flatbread stuffed with lentils
पनीर परांठा *paneer parantha* — flatbread stuffed with cheese
भरा नान *bhara naan* — stuffed naan bread
रुमाली रोटी *roomali roti* — a variety of Muslim bread
मिस्सी रोटी *missi roti* — bread made of chick pea flour
मक्के की रोटी *makki ki roti* — bread made of corn
मूली परांठा *mooli parantha* — bread stuffed with radish
तंदूरी रोटी *tandoori roti* — plain bread
नान *naan* — plain bread made of flour

Fruit

cherries	चेरी	*cherry*
plums	आलूबुखारा	*aaloobhukhara*
strawberries	स्ट्रॉबेरी	*strawberry*
pomegranates	अनार	*anaar*
apples	सेब	*seb*
peaches	आड़ू	*aadoo*
oranges	संतरा	*santra*
bananas	केला	*kela*
grapefruits	मौसमी	*mausmee*
grapes	अंगूर	*angoor*
honeydew melon	हनी ड्यू तरबूज	*honey dew tarbooz*
lychees	लीची	*leecheez*
longans	लोंगेन	*longen*
mangoes	आम	*aam*
pears	नाशपाती	*nashpati*
pineapple	अन्नास	*annanaas*
star fruit	स्टार फ्रूट	*star fruit*
tangerines	संतरा	*santra*
apricots	खूबानी	*khubaani*
lemon	नींबू	*neembu*

Paan - an ethnic Indian chew made of betel leaf, nuts and spices and/or tobacco - is usually served at the end of a meal and ceremonies such as weddings and receptions. It can be bought at nearly every street corner. It is believed to aid digestion and also acts as a mouth freshener. When **paan** is chewed, a red food dye stains the mouth red. Many people choose to spit it out rather than swallow it.

Dessert

scake	केक *cake*
frozen yougurt	ठंडा दही *thanda dahi*
ice-cream	आइसक्रीम *ice-cream*
vanilla	वनीला *vanilla*
chocolate	चॉकलेट *chocolate*
strawberry	स्ट्रॉबेरी *strawberry*
rabri - *sweet vermicelli mixed with almonds and pistachios*	रबड़ी *rabri*
rasmalai - *cottage*	रस मलाई *rasmalai*

cheese balls soaked
in flavored milk

rajbhog - *saffron-*   राज भोग *raj bhog*
flavored cottage cheese
balls stuffed with dry fruits

rasgulla - *cheese balls*   रसगुल्ला *rasgulla*
in syrup

jalebi - *crisp coils of*   जलेबी *jalebi*
fried batter in syrup

malpua - *fried flour*   मालपुआ *malpua*
flat bread dipped in
sugar syrup

gulabjamun - *a sweet*   गुलाब जामुन *gulabjamun*
ball made from milk
powder, fried in ghee,
and soaked in sugar
syrup

kheer - *a milky, sweet*   खीर *kheer*
semi-liquid dessert

phirni - *a smooth,*   फिरनी *phirni*
creamy pudding

Sauces & Condiments

Ketchup	केचप	*ketchup*
mustard	सरसों	*sarson*
pepper	काली मिर्च	*kaali mirch*
salt	नमक	*namak*

At the Market

Where are the trolleys/baskets?	ट्रॉली/बास्केट कहां हैं?	*trolley/basket kahan hain?*
Where is…?	…कहां है?	*…kahan hai?*
I'd like some of that/this.	मैं उसमें/इसमें से कुछ लेना चाहूंगा?	*main usmain/ismain se kuch lena chahoonga?*
Can I taste it?	क्या मैं इसे चख सकता हूं?	*kya main ise chakh sakta hoon?*
I'd like…	मैं…चाहूंगा	*main..chaahoonga*
a kilo/half kilo of…	…का एक किलो/आधा किलो	*…ka ek kilo/aadha kilo*
a liter of…	…का एक लीटर	*…ka ek liter*
a piece of…	…का एक टुकड़ा	*…ka ek tukda*
a slice of…	…की एक फांक	*..ki ek faank*
More./Less.	ज्यादा/कम	*zyada/ kum*
How much?	कितना?	*kitna*
Where do I pay?	मैं कहां भुगतान करूं?	*main kahan bhugtaan karoon?*

YOU MAY HEAR...

क्या मैं आपकी सहायता कर सकता हूं?　　Can I help you?
kya main aapki sahayata kar sakta hoon?

आप क्या पसंद करेंगे? *aap kya pasand karenge?*　What would you like?

और कुछ? *aur kuch?*　　Anything else?

यह...रुपये हैं। *yah...rupaye hain*　That's...rupee

Measurements in India are metric and that applies to the weight of food too. If you tend to think in pounds and ounces, it's worth brushing up on what the metric equivalent is before you go shopping for fruit and veg in markets and supermarkets. Five hundred grams, or half a kilo, is a common quantity to order, and that converts to just over a pound (17.65 ounces, to be precise).

YOU MAY SEE...

सर्वोत्तम यदि...द्वारा उपयोग होता है।	best if used by...
कैलोरी	calories
वसा मुक्त	fat free
रेफ्रिजरेटेड रखा जाए	keep refrigerated
...के कुछ कण हो सकते हैं।	may contain traces of...
माइक्रोवेवयोग्य	microwaveable
...द्वारा बिक्री	sell by...
शाकाहारियों के लिए उपयुक्त	suitable for vegetarians

| A bag, please. | कृपया, एक बैग दें। *kripya, ek bag dain* |
| I'm being helped. | मेरी सहायता की जा रही है। *meri sahayata ki jaa rahi hai* |

For Conversion Tables, see page 171.

In the Kitchen

bottle opener	बोतल ओपनर *bottle opener*
bowl	कटोरा *katora*
can opener	कैन ओपनर *can opener*
corkscrew	कॉर्क स्क्रू *corkscrew*
cup	कप *cup*
fork	कांटा *kaanta*
frying pan	फ़्राइंग पैन *frying pan*
glass	ग्लास *glass*
(steak) knife	(स्टीक) चाकू *(steak) chakoo*
measuring cup/	नापने वाला कप/चम्मच
spoon	*naapne wala cup/chammach*
napkin	नैपकिन *napkin*
plate	प्लेट *plate*
pot	हंडिया *handiya*
spatula	स्पैचुला *spatula*
spoon	चम्मच *chammach*

Drinks

ESSENTIAL

The wine list/drink menu, please.	कृपया, केचप सूची/ ड्रिंक मेनू दें। *kripya, sharab suchi/ drink menu dein*
What do you recommend?	आप क्या सुझाव देते हैं? *aap kya sujhav dete hain*
I'd like a bottle/glass of red/white wine.	मैं लाल/सफेद वाइन का एक बोतल/ग्लास लेना चाहूंगा *main lal/safed wine ka ek bottle/glass lena chahoonga*
The house wine, please.	कृपया, हाउस वाइन दें। *kripya, house wine dein*
Another bottle/glass, please.	कृपया, एक और बोतल/ग्लास दें। *kripya, ek aur bottle/glass dein*
I'd like a local beer.	मैं स्थानीय बीयर पसंद करुंगा। *main sthaniya beer pasand karoonga*
Can I buy you a drink?	क्या मैं पेय खरीद सकता हूं। *kya main peya kharid sakta hoon*
Cheers!	चीयर्स! *cheers*
A coffee/tea, please.	कृपया, एक कॉफी/चाय दें *kripya, ek coffee/chay*
Black.	काली *kaali*
With...	...के साथ ...*ke saath*
milk	दूध *doodh*
sugar	चीनी *chini*
artificial sweetener	कृत्रिम स्वीटनर *kritrim sweetener*
A..., please.	कृपया, एक...दें *kripya, ek...dein*
juice	जूस *juice*
soda	सोडा *soda*
(sparkling/still) water	(स्पार्कलिंग/स्टिल) वॉटर *(sparkling/still) water*

Non-alcoholic Drinks

black tea	काली चाय *kaali chai*
coffee	कॉफी *coffee*
green tea	ग्रीन टी *green tea*
hot chocolate	हॉट चॉकलेट *hot chocolate*
iced coffee	आईस्ड कॉफी *iced coffee*
iced tea	आईस्ड टी *iced tea*
jasmine tea	जैसमीन टी *jasmine tea*
lemonade	लेमोनेड *lemonade*
lychee tea	लीची टी *leechee tea*
(sparkling/still) water	(स्पार्कलिंग/स्टिल) वॉटर *(sparkling/still) water*
juice	फलों का रस *phalon ka rus*
lassi	लस्सी *lassi*
milk	दूध *dhoodh*
milkshake	मिल्क शेक *milk shake*
orange juice	शेक का रस *santra ka rus*
soda water	सोडा पानी *soda paani*
tonic water	टॉनिक पानी *tonic paani*
tea	चाय *chai*

Chai is the Indian word for tea. More specifically, it is a blended beverage of mixed spices, milk and honey.
Tea is a very popular drink and you can find a tea stand on every corner. South Indians favor coffee, usually with loads of milk and sugar. Soda or soft drinks such as Seven-Up (सेवन-अप *seven-up*) and Coca Cola (कोका-कोला *coca-cola*) are the same as they are in English.

YOU MAY HEAR...

क्या मैं आपके लिए पेय ले लूं?	Can I get you a drink?
kya main aapke liye peya le loon	
दूध या चीनी के साथ? *doodh ya chini ke saath*	With milk or sugar?
स्पार्कलिंग या स्टिल वॉटर *sparkling ya still water*	Sparkling or still water?

Apéritifs, Cocktails & Liqueurs

brandy	ब्रांडी	*brandy*
gin	जिन	*gin*
rum	रम	*rum*
scotch	स्कॉच	*scotch*
tequila	टकीला	*taquila*
vodka	वोदका	*vodka*
whisky	व्हिस्की	*whisky*

Beer

…beer	…बीयर	*beer*
Bottled/Draft	बॉटल्ड/ड्राफ्ट	*bottled/draft*
Dark/Light	गाढ़ी/हल्की	*gaadhi/halki*
Lager/Pilsener	लेजर/लिपसेनर	*lager/lipsener*
Local/Imported	लोकल/इम्पोर्टेड	*local/imported*
Non-alcoholic	गैर एल्कोहलिक	*gair alcoholic*

86

Most brands of beer are straightforward pilsners with around
5% alcohol. Outside the cities and tourist centers, you may
struggle to find a beer cold enough to quench your thirst; make
sure you feel the bottle before the waiter opens it. Most travelers like
Kingfisher, which is available nationwide. Royal Challenge, Kalyani, and
Sand Piper are popular.

Wine

…wine	वाइन	*wine*
Red/White	लाल/सफेद	*lal/safed*
House/Table	हाउस/टेबल	*house/table*
Dry/Sweet	सूखी/मीठी	*sukhi/meethi*
Sparkling	स्पार्कलिंग	*sparkling*
champagne	शैंपेन	*champagne*
dessert wine	डेज़र्ट वाइन	*dessert wine*

On the Menu

एबलोन *abalone*	abalone [sea snails]
एग बिरयानी *egg biryani*	flavored egg rice
फ्राई *fries*	french fries [chips]
खीर *kheer*	a milky, sweet semi-liquid dessert
खीरा *kheera*	cucumber
खूबानी *khubaani*	apricots
रुमाली रोटी *roomali roti*	very thin flatbread, often known as "hankerchief" bread
ढोकला *dokhla*	steamed cubes of ground rice lentils, seasoned with mustard seeds and red chili
झींगा *jheenga*	lobster
इडली *idli*	steamed rice cakes
बंदगोभी *bundhgobi*	cabbage
बकरा *bakra*	goat
बड़ा श्रिम्प *bada shrimp*	large shrimp
बछड़े का मांस/वील *bachde ka maans/veal*	veal
बैंबू शूट्स *bamboo shoots*	bamboo shoots
बैंगन *baingun*	eggplant [aubergine]
बेबी स्क्विड *baby squid*	baby squid
बटर चिकन *butter chicken*	boneless chicken simmered in butter and creamy rich tomato sauce
बत्तख *batakh*	duck
ब्रेड *bread*	bread
ब्रेड पकौड़ा *bread pakoda*	bread slices dipped in spicy chick pea flour batter and deep fried

तंदूरी चिकन *tandoori chicken* — chicken grilled in oven

कृत्रिम मक्खन
kritreem makhan — margarine

कौड *cod* — cod

कोकोनट उत्पम
coconut uttapum — flat rice bread stuffed with coconut

कुकीज [बिस्कुट]
cookies [biscuit] — cookies [biscuits]

कुकुरमुत्ता
kukurmutta — mushrooms

केक *cake* — cake

कैट फिश *catfish* — catfish

केला *kela* — bananas

क्लैम्स *clamps* — clams

कलेजी *kalejee* — liver

मक्खन *makhan* — butter

मक्के की रोटी *makki ki roti* — bread made of corn

मीठी लाल मिर्च
meethee lal mirch — sweet red peppers

मशरूम सूप *mushroom soup* — mushroom soup

मौसमी *mausmee* — grapefruits

मालपुआ *malpua*	fried flour flat bread dipped in sugar syrup
मसाला डोसा *masala dosa*	fried dish made of lentils, rice and potato
मुसेल्स *mussels*	mussels
मेमना/लैंब *memnaa/lamb*	lamb
मटर *mutter*	peas
मटर *mutter*	snow peas [mangetout]
मटर मशरूम *mutter mushroom*	mushroom and peas cooked in a curry sauce
मटन बिरयानी *mutton biryani*	flavored mutton rice
मटन दहीवाला *mutton dahiwalla*	mutton cooked in curd
मूंगफली *moongphali*	peanuts
मूली परांठा *mooli parantha*	bread stuffed with radish
मलाई *malaai*	cream
मिठा और खट्टा *meetha aur khutta*	sweet and sour chicken
मिक्स उत्पम *mixed uttapam*	flat rice bread stuffed with mixed vegetables

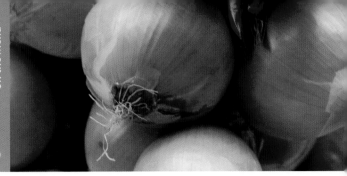

मिस्सी रोटी *missi roti*	bread made of chick pea flour
श्रिम्प *shrimp*	shrimp
स्प्रिंग कबूतर *spring kabootar*	spring pigeon
चिकन *chicken*	chicken
चिकन बिरयानी *chicken biryani*	fragrant chicken rice
चिकन हॉट एंड *chicken hot and sour soup*	chicken hot and sour soup
चिकन पालक *chicken paalak*	chicken spinach soup
चिकन स्वीट कॉर्न सूप *chicken sweet corn soup*	chicken sweetcorn soup
चिकन सूप *chicken soup*	chicken soup
फिरनी *phirni*	a smooth, creamy pudding
फिलैट स्टीक *fillet steak*	fillet steak
हंस *huns*	goose
हरे सेम *hare sem*	green beans
हॉट डॉग *hot dog*	hot dog
हैमबर्गर *hamburger*	hamburger
हेरिंग *herring*	herring
हनी ड्यू तरबूज *honey dew tarbooz*	honeydew melon
भरा नान *bhara naan*	stuffed naan bread
भुनी बत्तख *bhuni batakh*	roast duck

भेल पूरी *bhel puri*	puffed rice mixed with veg. and sauces
प्याज *pyaaz*	onion
पाइनेपल बत्तख *pineapple batakh*	pineapple duck
शार्क का पंख *shark ka pankh*	shark's fin
शाही पनीर *shahi paneer*	cottage cheese simmered in butter and creamy rich tomato sauce
शतावरी *shatawari*	asparagus
पालक *paalak*	spinach
पनीर *paneer*	cheese
पनीर टिक्का मसाला *paneer tikka masala*	cottage cheese grilled in the oven
पनीर पकौड़ा *paneer pakoda*	bread slices stuffed with cheese dipped in spicy chickpea flour batter and deep fried
पनीर पकौड़ा *paneer pakoda*	bread slices stuffed with cheese dipped in spicy chickpea flour batter and deep fried

पनीर परांठा *paneer parantha* — flatbread stuffed with cheese

पनीर उत्पम *paneer uttapam* — flat rice bread stuffed with cheese

रबड़ी *rabri* — sweet vermicelli mixed with almonds and pistachios

रम्प स्टीक *rump steak* — rump steak

रोगन जोश *rogan josh* — mutton cooked with the most intensely hot and fragrant spices

राज कचौड़ी *raj kachori* — deep fried wheat pastry filled with potato, chick peas, and spices

राज भोग *rajbhog* — saffron-flavored cottage cheese balls stuffed with dry fruits

राजमा मसाला *rajma masala* — red kidney beans cooked in curry

रस मलाई *rasmalai* — cottage cheese balls soaked in flavored milk

रस गुल्ला *rasgulla* — cheese balls in syrup

रवा मसाला डोसा — semolina pancake filled with
rava masala dosa — potato masala

संतरा *santra* — oranges

संतरा *santra* — tangerines

सब्जी का सूप *subjee kaa soup* — vegetable soup

सब्जी तालू मियन *subjee taalu miyan* — vegetable talu mein

स्कालोप्स *scallops* — scallops

समोसा *samosa* — stuffed triangle-shaped pastries filled with mildly spiced potatoes

समुद्री बैस *samudri baas* — sea bass

सीक कबाब — minced mutton or chicken
seekh kabab — cooked in oven

सरलोयन स्टीक *sirloin steak* — sirloin steak

सादा परांठा *saada* — flatbread

सोल *sole* — sole

सॉसेज़ *sausage* — sausages

सैंडविच *sandwich* — sandwich

सेब *seb* — apples

सेम *sem* — beans

स्टार फ़्रूट *star fruit* — star fruit

स्टीक *steak* — steak

स्ट्रॉबेरी *strawberry* — strawberries

सलाद *salad* — lettuce

दही *dahi* — yogurt

दही भल्ला *dahi bhalla* — pastries made from lentils, served with yogurt and chutneys

छोले भटूरे *choley bhature* — seasoned garbanzo beans [chickpeas] served with fresh fried bread

दाल मख्नी *dal makhni* — whole black lentils sautéed in garlic and fresh tomatoes

दूध *dhoodh* — milk

व्हाईट बैट *whitebait* — whitebait

वेज हॉट एंड सॉर सूप *veg hot and sour soup* — veg. hot & sour soup

वेज स्वीट कॉर्न सूप *veg sweet corn soup* — veg. sweet corn soup

वेजीटेबल बिरयानी *vegetable biryani* — flavored vegetable rice

चावल *chawal* — rice

चावल दलिया *chawal daleeyaa* — rice porridge

चाट *chaat* — yogurt and potatoes with sauces

चॉकलेट *chocolate* — chocolate

चॉप्स *chops* — chops

चेरी *cherry* — cherries

फूलगोभी *phoolgobi* — broccoli

तंदूरी रोटी *tandoori roti* — plain bread

जीरा आलू *jeera aaloo* — potato cooked in different spices

जलकुंभी *julkumbhi* — watercress

जलेबी *jalebi* — crisp coils of fried batter in syrup

नरगिसी कोफ्ता *nargisi kofta* — minced meat mixed with spicy curry

नाशपाती *nashpati* — pears

नान *naan* — plain bread made of flour

नवरत्न कोरमा *navratan korma* — nine vegetables dish

अंकुरित मटर *ankurit mutter* — pea sprouts

अंकुरित सेम *ankurit sem* — bean sprouts

अंगूर *angoor* — grapes

टर्की *turkey* — turkey

टमाटर *tamater* — tomato

टमाटर का सूप *tamater kaa soup*	tomato soup
टमाटर और तुलसी *tamater aur tulsi*	tomato & basil soup
टी-बोन स्टीक *tee bone steak*	T-bone steak
आइसक्रीम *ice cream*	ice cream
आम *aam*	mangoes
आड़ू *aadoo*	peaches
ओएस्टर *oyster*	oysters
आलू *aaloo*	potatoes
आलू की टिक्की *aloo ki tikki*	stuffed mashed potato cakes
आलू चिप्स [कुरकुरा] *aaloo chips [kurkuraa]*	potato chips [crisps]
आलू परांठा *aaloo parantha*	flatbread stuffed with mashed potato
आलूबुख़ारा *aaloobhukhara*	plums
टुना *tuna*	tuna
ट्राउट *trout*	trout
अजवाइन *ajwain*	celery
अनार *anaar*	pomegranates
अनन्नास *annanaas*	pineapple
गो मांस *go maans*	beef

गोल गप्पा *gol guppa*	fried puffs of dough filled with veg. and spicy sauce
गाजर *gajar*	carrots
गुर्दा *gurda*	kidneys
गुलाब जामुन *gulabjamun*	a sweet ball made from milk powder, fried in ghee, and soaked in sugar syrup
ग्रास कार्प *grass carp*	grass carp
लीची *leecheez*	lychees
लोंगेन *longen*	longans
लाल स्नैपर *lal snapper*	red snapper

People

Conversation

ESSENTIAL

Hello!/Hi!	नमस्ते!	*namaste!*
How are you?	आप कैसे हैं?	*aap kaise hain?*
Fine, thanks.	अच्छा, धन्यवाद।	*achcha dhanyavad*
Excuse me!	माफ़ करिए!	*Maaf kariye!*
Do you speak English?	क्या आप अंग्रेजी बोलते / बोलती हैं?	*kya aap angrezi bolte m / bolti f hain?*
What's your name?	आपका क्या नाम है?	*aapka kya naam hai?*
My name is...	मेरा नाम...है।	*mera naam...hai*
Nice to meet you.	आपसे मिलकर खुशी हुई।	*aapse milkar khusi hui*
Where are you from?	आप कहां से हैं?	*aap kahan se hain?*
I'm from the U.K./U.S	मैं यू.के./यू.एस. से हूं।	*main U.K./U.S. se hoon*
What do you do for a living?	आप जीवनयापन के लिए क्या करते हैं?	*aap jivanyapan ke liye kya karte hai?*
I work for...	मैं...के लिए काम करता हूं।	*main...ke liye kaam karta hoon*
I'm a student.	मैं छात्र हूं।	*main chhatra hoon*
I'm retired.	मैं सेवानिवृत्त हूं।	*main sevanivritta hoon*
Do you like...?	क्या आपको...पसंद है।	*kya aapko...pasand hai?*
Goodbye.	अलविदा।	*alvida*
See you later.	फिर मिलते हैं।	*fir milte hain*

Hindi uses numerous English loan words, which makes it easy for English speakers to build their vocabulary quickly. Note though that the pronunciation of many of the loan words is different in Hindi. For many Indians, English is their first language and English is widely spoken in India.

Language Difficulties

Do you speak English?	क्या आप अंग्रेजी बोलते हैं?
	kya aap angrezi bolte hain
Does anyone here speak English?	क्या यहा कोई अंग्रेजी बोलता है?
	kya yahan koi angreji boltaa hai?
I don't speak (much) Hindi.	मैं (बहुत) हिंदी नहीं बोलता/बोलती हूं|
	main (bahut) hindi nahin bolta m/bolti f hoon
Could you speak more slowly?	क्या आप धीरे बोल सकते हैं?
	kya aap dheere bol sakte hain?
Could you repeat that?	क्या आप दुबारा बोल सकते हैं?
	kya aap dobaara bol sakte hain?
Excuse me? [Pardon?]	माफ कीजिए? *maaf kijiye?*
Please write it down.	कृपया लिखें| *kripyaa likhen*
Can you translate this for me?	क्या आप इसे मेरे लिए अनुवाद कर सकते हैं?
	kya aap isse mere liye anuvaad kur sakte hain?
What does this/that mean?	इसका क्या मतलब है?
	iska kya mutlub hai?
I understand.	मैं समझ गया| *main samajh gaya*
I don't understand.	मुझे समझ में नहीं आया|
	mujhe samajh mein nahin aaya
Do you understand?	क्या आपको समझ में आया?
	kya aapko samajh mein aaya?

YOU MAY HEAR...

मैं केवल थोड़ी अंग्रेजी बोलता / बोलती हूं।
main keval thodi angrezi bolta m / bolti f hoon
मैं अंग्रेजी नहीं बोलता / बोलती हूं।
main angrezi nahin bolta m / bolti f hoon

I only speak a little English.
I don't speak English.

Making Friends

Hello!	हैलो/नमस्ते! *Hello/namaste!*
Good afternoon.	नमस्कार। *namaskaar*
Good evening.	नमस्कार। *namaskaar*
My name is...	मेरा नाम...है। *mera naam...hai*
What's your name?	आपका नाम क्या है? *aapka naam kya hai?*
I'd like to introduce you to...	मैं आपको...से मिलवाना चाहता/चाहती हूं। *main aapko...se milwana chahta/chati hoon*
Pleased to meet you.	आपसे मिलकर खुशी हुई। *aapse milkar khusi hui*
How are you?	आप कैसे हैं? *aap kaise hain?*
Fine, thanks. And you?	अच्छा, धन्यवाद! और आप? *achcha, dhanyavad. Aur aap?*

There are a few rules of etiquette that should be respected when meeting up with locals: always remove your shoes before entering someone's house, or a place of worship. When eating with your fingers, remember to only use your right hand and don't point with your index finger as this may be considered a sign of disrespect – use either your extended hand or your chin.

Travel Talk

I'm here...	मैं यहां...हूं	*main yahan...hoon*
on business	व्यवसाय पर	*vyavsaaya par*
on vacation [holiday]	अवकाश [छुट्टी] पर	*avakaash [chhutti] par*
studying	पढ़ने के लिए	*padhne ke liye*
I'm staying for...	मैं...के लिए रह रहा हूं	*main...ke liye raha raha hoon*
I've been here...	मैं यहां...से हूं	*main yahan...se hoon*
a day	एक दिन	*ek din*
a week	एक सप्ताह	*ek saptaah*
a month	एक माह	*ek maah*
Where are you from?	आप कहां से हैं?	*aap kahan se hain?*

I'm from... मैं...से हूं *main...se hoon*

For Business Travel, see page 141.

Personal

Who are you with?	आप किसके साथ हैं?	*aap kiske saath hain?*
I'm here alone.	मैं यहां अकेला / अकेली हूं	
	*main yahan akela **m** / akeli **f** hoon*	
I'm with...	मैं...के साथ हूं *main...ke saath hoon*	
my husband/wife	अपने पति/पत्नी *apne pati/patni*	
my boyfriend	अपने पुरुष/महिला मित्र	
/girlfriend	*apne purush mitra/mahila mitra*	
a friend	एक मित्र *ek mitra*	
friends	मित्रों *mitron*	
a colleague	एक सहकर्मी *ek sahkarmi*	
colleagues	सहकर्मियों *sahkarmiyon*	
When's your birthday?	आपका जन्मदिन कब है? *aapka janmdin kab hai?*	
How old are you?	आप कितने साल के / की हैं?	
	*aap kitne saal ke **m** / ki **f** hain?*	
I'm...	मैं...हूं *main...hoon*	
Are you married?	क्या आप विवाहित हैं? *kya aap vivahit hain?*	
I'm...	मैं...हूं *main...hoon*	
single/in a	एकल/एक रिश्ते में *ekal/ ek rishte main*	
relationship		
engaged	इंगेज *engage*	
married	विवाहित *vivahit*	
divorced	तलाकशुदा *talakshuda*	
separated	अलग *alag*	
widowed	विधवा/विधुर *vidhwa/vidhur*	
Do you have children/	क्या आपके बच्चे/नाती-पोते हैं?	
grandchildren?	*kya aapke bachche/nati-pote hain?*	

For Numbers, see page 165.

Work & School

What do you do for a living?	आप जीवनयापन के लिए क्या करते / करती हैं? *aap jivanyapan ke liye kya karte m / karti f hain?*
What are you studying?	आप क्या पढ़ रहे/रही हैं? *aap kya padh rahe/rahi hain?*
I'm studying French.	मैं फ्रेंच पढ़ रहा/रही हूं। *main French padh raha/rahi hoon*
I...	मैं... *main...*
work full-/ part-time	पूर्णकालिक-/ अंशकालिक काम करता / करती हूं। *main poornkalik-/anshkalik kaam karta m / karti f hoon*
am unemployed	बेरोजगार हूं। *berozgaar hoon*
work at home ?	घर पर काम करता / करती हूं। *ghar par kaam karta m / karti f hoon?*
Who do you work for?	आप किसके लिए काम करते / करती हैं। *aap kiske liye kaam karte m / karti f hain?*
I work for...	मैं...के लिए काम करता / करती हूं। *main...ke liye kaam karta m / karti f hoon*
Here's my business card.	यह मेरा बिजनेस कार्ड है। *yah mera business card hai*

For Business Travel, see page 141.

Weather

What's the forecast?	मौसम की भविष्यवाणी क्या है? *mausam ki bhavishyawadi kya hai?*
What beautiful/ terrible weather!	कितना सुहाना/खराब मौसम है! *Kitna suhana/kharab mausam ha!i*
It's...	बहुत...है *bahut...hai*
cool/warm	ठंड/गर्म *thand/garm*
cold/hot	सर्दी/गरमी *sardi/garmi*
rainy/sunny	धूप/बरसात *dhoop/barsaat*
snowy/icy	बर्फबारी/बर्फीला *barfbaari/barfilaa*
Do I need a jacket/ an umbrella?	मुझे एक जैकेट/एक छाते की आवश्यकता है? *mujhe ek jacket/ek chate ki aavashyakta hai?*

For Temperature, see page 172.

ESSENTIAL

Would you like to go out for a drink/ dinner?	क्या आप पीने/खाने के लिए बाहर जाना पसंद करेंगे / करेंगी? *kya aap peene/khane ke liye bahar jaana pasand karenge m / karengi f?*
What are your plans for tonight/tomorrow?	आज रात/कल के लिए आपकी क्या योजना है? *aaj raat/kal ke liye aapki kya yojna hai?*
Can I have your (phone) number?	क्या मुझे आपका (फोन) नंबर मिल सकता है? *kya mujhe aapka phone number mil sakta hai?*
Can I join you?	क्या मैं आपसे जुड़ सकता / सकती हूं? *kya main aapse jud sakta m / sakti f hoon?*
Can I buy you a drink?	क्या मैं आपके लिए एक पेय खरीद सकता / सकती हूं? *kya main aapke liye ek peya khareed sakta m / sakti f hoon?*
I love you.	मैं आपसे प्यार करता / करती हूं! *main aapse pyar karta m / karti f hoon*

The Dating Game

Would you like to go out...?	क्या आप...बाहर जाना पसंद करेंगे / करेंगी? *kya aap...bahar jaana pasand karenge m / karengi f?*
for coffee	कॉफी के लिए *coffee ke liye*
for a drink	पीने के लिए *peene ke liye*
to dinner	खाने के लिए *khane ke liye*
What are your plans for...?	...के लिए आपकी क्या योजना है? *...ke liye aapki kya yojna hai?*
today	आज *aaj*
tonight	आज रात *aaj raat*
tomorrow	कल *kal*
this weekend	इस सप्ताहांत *is saptahant*

Where would you like to go?	आप कहां जाना पसंद करेंगे / करेंगी?
	aap kahan jaana pasand karenge m / karengi f ?
I'd like to go to…	मैं…जाना पसंद करूंगी / करूंगा।
	main. . .jana pasand karoongi f / karoonga m
Do you like…?	क्या आप…पसंद करती / करते हैं?
	kya aap. . .pasand karti f / karte m hain?
Can I have your phone number/ email?	क्या मुझे आपका फोन नंबर/ईमेल मिल सकता है?
	kya mjhe aapka phone number/email mil sakta hai?
Are you on Facebook /Twitter?	क्या आप फेसबुक/ट्विटर पर हैं?
	kya aap facebook/twitter par hain?
Can I join you?	क्या मैं आपसे जुड़ सकता / सकती हूं?
	kya main aapse jud sakta m / sakti f hoon?
You're very attractive.	आप बहुत आकर्षक हैं। *aap bahut aakarshak hain*
Let's go somewhere quieter.	आओ कहीं और शांति में चलें।
	aao kahin aur shanty main chalein

Accepting & Rejecting

I'd love to.	मैं पसंद करूंगा / करूंगी।
	main pasand karoonga m / karoongi f
Where should we meet?	हमें कहां मिलना चाहिए? *hamein kahan milna chahiye?*
I'll meet you at	मैं तुम्हें बार/अपने होटल में मिलूंगा / मिलूंगी।

the bar/your hotel.	*main tumhe bar/apne hotel main miloonga* **m** / *miloongi* **f**
I'll come by at…	मैं…तक आ जाऊंगा / जाऊंगी ।
	main…tak aa jaoonga **m** / *jaoongi* **f**
I'm busy.	मैं व्यस्त हूं। *main vyasta hoon*
I'm not interested.	मैं इच्छुक नहीं हूं। *main ichchhuk hoon*
Leave me alone.	मुझे अकेला छोड़ दो। *mujhe akela chod do*
Stop bothering me!	मुझे शांति करना बंद करो!
	Mujhe pareshan karna band karo!

Getting Intimate

Can I hug/kiss you?	क्या मैं तुम्हें गले लगा/चूम सकता / सकता हूं?
	kya main tumhe gale laga/chum sakta **m** / *sakti* **f** *hoon?*
Yes.	हां। *haan*
No.	नहीं। *nahin*
Stop!	रुको! *ruko*
I love you.	मैं तुम्हें प्यार करता/करती हूं
	main tumhe pyaar karta hoon

Sexual Preferences

Are you gay?	क्या तुम समलैंगिक हो? *kya tum samlaingik ho?*
I'm…	मैं…हूं। *main…hoon*
heterosexual	विषमलैंगिक *vishamlaingik*
homosexual	समलैंगिक *samlaingik*
bisexual	उभयलिंगी *ubhayingi*
Do you like men/	क्या आप पुरुष/महिलाओं को पसंद करते / करती हैं?
women?	*kya aap purush/mahilaon ko pasand karte* **m** /*karti hain* **f** ?

Kissing and embracing in public is frowned upon; in rural areas, even men and women holding hands can provoke curious stares (although the sight of Indian men holding hands is common).

Leisure Time

Sightseeing

ESSENTIAL

Where's the tourist information office?	पर्यटक सूचना कार्यालय कहां है? *paryatan soochna karyalaya kahan hai?*
What are the main sights?	प्रमुख स्थल क्या हैं? *pramukh sthal kya hain?*
Do you offer tours in English?	क्या आप अंग्रेजी में यात्रा की पेशकश करते हैं? *kya aap angrezi main yatra ki peshkash karte hain?*
Can I have a map/guide?	क्या मुझे मानचित्र/गाइड मिल सकता / सकती है? *kya mujhe manchitra/guide mil sakta m / sakti f hai?*

Tourist Information

Do you have information on...?	क्या आपके पास...पर सूचना है? *kya aapke paas...par soochna hai?*
Can you recommend...?	क्या आप... सुझाव दे सकते हैं? *kya aap sujhav de sakte hain?*
a bus tour	एक बस यात्रा का *ek bus yatra ka*
an excursion to...	भ्रमण के लिए...का *bhraman ke liye...ka*
a tour of...	एक ...की यात्रा का *ek...ki yatra ka*

For Seeing the Sights, see page 111.

The Ministry of Tourism has a good website (**www.incredibleindia.org**), with a lot of useful information on obtaining visas, places to visit and tour operators.

YOU MAY HEAR...

सौभाग्य! बहुत सारी शुभकामनाएं!
saubhagya! bahut saari shubhkaamnay
यात्रा मंगलमय हो! *yatraa mangalmay ho!*
यह आपके लिए *yeh aapke liye*

Good luck!/All the best!

Have a good trip!
Here you are.

On Tour

I'd like to go on the excursion to...	मैं...पर भ्रमण के लिए जाना चाहूंगा / चाहूंगी *main... par bhraman ke liye jana chahoonga **m** / chahoongi **f***
When's the next tour?	अगली यात्रा कब है? *agli yaatra kab hai?*
Are there tours in English?	क्या यात्राएं अंग्रेजी में हैं? *kya yaatrayen angrezi main hain?*
Is there an English guide book/ audio guide?	क्या कोई अंग्रेजी गाइड बुक/ऑडियो गाइड है? *kya koi angrezi guide book/audio guide hai?*
What time do we leave/return?	किस समय हम निकलेंगे/वापस आएंगे? *kis samay hum nikalenge/vapas aayenge?*
We'd like to see...	मैं...देखना चाहूंगा / चाहूंगी। *main dekhna chahoonga **m** / chahoongi **f***

Can we stop here...? क्या हम यहां...रुक सकते हैं? *kya hum yahan...ruk sakte hain?*

    to take photos फोटो लेने के लिए *photo lene ke liye*

    for souvenirs स्मृति चिन्ह के लिए *smiriti chinh ke liye*

    for the toilets शौचालय के लिए *shauchalaya ke liye*

Is it disabled-accessible? क्या यह विकलांग-सुलभ है? *kya yahaviklang-sulabh hai?*

For Tickets, see page 19.

Seeing the Sights

Where's...? ...कहां है? *kahan hai?*

    the battleground युद्धभूमि *yudhbhoomi*

    the botanical garden बोटैनिकल गार्डन *botanical garden*

    the burial site अंत्येष्टि स्थल *antyeshthi sthal*

    the castle किला *kila*

    the downtown शहर *shahar*

    the elephant safari हाथी सफारी *haathi safari*

    the fountain फव्वारा *favvara*

    the library पुस्तकालय *pustkalaya*

    the market बाज़ार *bazaar*

    the museum संग्रहालय *sangrahalaya*

    the national park राष्ट्रीय उद्यान *rashtriya udyan*

    the old town पुराना शहर *purana shahar*

the opera house	ओपेरा हाउस	*opera house*
the palace	महल	*mahal*
the park	पार्क	*park*
the ruins	पुराने अवशेष	*purane avshesh*
the safari park	सफारी पार्क	*safari park*
the shopping area	शॉपिंग क्षेत्र	*shopping ksehtra*
the shrine	तीर्थस्थान	*tirthsthan*
the tiger reserve	बाघ अभयारण्य	*baagh abhayaranya*
the tomb	मकबरा	*makbara*
the town square	शहर चौक	*shahar chowk*
Can you show me on the map?	क्या तुम मुझ मानचित्र पर दिखा सकते हो?	*kya tum mujhe maanchitra par dikha sakte ho?*
It's...	यह...है	*yah...hai*
amazing	अद्भुत	*adbhut*
beautiful	सुंदर	*sundar*
boring	बोरिंग	*boring*
interesting	दिलचस्प	*dilchasp*
magnificent	शानदार	*shaandaar*
romantic	रूमानी	*rumani*
strange	अनोखा	*anokha*
terrible	भयानक	*bhayanak*
ugly	कुरूप	*kurup*

I (don't) like it. मुझे यह पसंद (नहीं) है *mujhe yah pasand (nahin) hai*

For Asking Directions, see page 33.

Religious Sites

Where's...?	...कहां हैं? *kahan hai?*
the cathedral	बड़ा गिरजाघर *bada girjaghar*
the Catholic/ Protestant church	कैथोलिक/प्रोटेस्टेंट गिरजाघर *Catholic/ Protestant girjaghar*
the mosque	मस्जिद *masjid*
the shrine	तीर्थस्थल *tirthsthal*
the synagogue	यहूदी उपसनागृह *yahudi upasanagrih*
the temple	मंदिर *mandir*
What time is the service?	सेवा का क्या समय है? *seva ka kya samay hai?*

Whenever you enter religious grounds, you must remove your shoes and socks. Proper clothing should also be worn at a temple: no short skirts for women and no brief shorts. Leather goods of any kind should not be taken into temples as they are regarded as impure and may cause offence.

Shopping

ESSENTIAL

Where's the market/ mall?	बाज़ार/मॉल कहां है? *bazaar/mall kahan hai?*
I'm just looking.	मैं बस देख रहा / रही हूं! *main bas dekh raha **m** / rahi **f** hoon*
Can you help me?	क्या आप मेरी सहायता कर सकते हैं? *kya aap meri sahayta kar sakte hain?*
I'm being helped.	मेरी सहायता की जा रही है। *meri sahayta ki jaa rahi hai*
How much?	कितनी/कितना? *kitni/kitna?*
That one, please.	कृपया, वो वाला/वाली। *kripya, voh wala/wali*
That's all.	वो सभी। *voh sabhi*
Where can I pay?	मैं कहां भुगतान कर सकता / सकती हूं? *main bhugtaan kar sakta **m** / sakti **f** hoon?*
I'll pay in cash/by credit card.	मैं नकद में/क्रेडिट कार्ड से भुगतान करूंगा / करूंगी। *main nakad main/credit se bhugtan karoonga **m** / karoongi **f***
A receipt, please.	कृपया, रसीद दें। *kripya rasid dein*

At the Shops

Where's...?	...कहां है? *... kahan hai?*
the antiques store	एंटीक स्टोर *antiques store*
the bakery	बेकरी *bakery*
the bank	बैंक *bank*
the bookstore	बुकस्टोर *bookstore*
the clothing store	कपड़ों का स्टोर *kapadon ka store*

the delicatessen	डेली स्टोर *daily store*
the department	डिपार्टमेंट *department*
the gift shop	गिफ्ट शॉप *gift shop*
the health food store	हेल्थ फूड स्टोर *health food store*
the jeweler	जौहरी *jhauhari*
the liquor store [off-licence]	शराब की दुकान *sharab ki dukan*
the market	बाज़ार *bazaar*
the music store	म्यूज़िक स्टोर *music store*
the pastry shop	पेस्ट्री शॉप *pastry shop*
the pharmacy	दवा की दुकान *dawa ki dukan*
the produce [grocery] store	उत्पाद [किराना] स्टोर *utpaad [kirana] store*
the shoe store	जूता स्टोर *juta store*
the shopping mall	शॉपिंग मॉल *shopping mall*
the souvenir store	स्मृति चिन्ह स्टोर *smriti chinha store*
the supermarket	सुपरमार्केट *supermarket*
the tobacconist	तंबाकू बेचने वाला *tambaakoo bechne wala*
the toy store	खिलौना स्टोर *khilauna store*

YOU MAY HEAR...

क्या मैं आपकी सहायता कर सकता / सकती हूं? Can I help you?
*kya main aapki sahayta kar sakta **m** / sakti **f** hoon ?*

थोड़ा ठहरिये। *thoda thahariye*   One moment.

आप क्या पसंद करेंगे? *aap kyaa pasand karenge?* What would you like?

कुछ और? *kuch aur?*   Anything else?

Ask an Assistant

When do you open/close?	आप कब खुले/बंद रहते हैं? *aap kab khule/band rahte hain?*
the cashier	खजांची *khajaanchi*
the escalator	एस्केलेटर *escalator*
the elevator [lift]	लिफ्ट *lift*
the fitting room	फिटिंग रूम *fitting room*
the store directory	स्टोर डायरेक्ट्री *store directory*
Can you help me?	क्या आप मेरी सहायता कर सकते हैं? *kya aap meri sahayta kar sakte hain?*
I'm just looking.	मैं बस देख रहा हूं। *main bas dekh raha hoon*
I'm being helped.	मेरी सहायता की जा रही है। *meri sahayta ki jaa rahi hai*
Do you have...?	क्या आपके पास... है? *kya aapke paas...hai?*
Can you show me...?	क्या आप मुझे...दिखा सकते हैं? *kya aap mujhe...dikha sakte hain?*
Can you ship/wrap it?	क्या आप इसे भेज/लपेट सकते हैं? *kya aap ise bhej/lapet sakte hain?*
How much?	कितना? *kitna*
That's all.	बस इतना ही। *bas itna hi*

For Souvenirs, see page 128.

Personal Preferences

I'd like something…	मैं कुछ…पसंद करूंगा / करूंगी
	main kuch…pasand karoonga **m** / *karoongi* **f**
cheap/expensive	सस्ता/महंगा *sasta/mahnga*
larger/smaller	बड़ा/छोटा *bada/chota*
from this region	इस क्षेत्र से *is kshetra se*
Around…rupee.	लगभग…रुपये *lagbhag…rupee*
Is it real?	क्या यह असली है? *kya yah asli hai?*
Can you show me this/that?	क्या मुझे आप यह/वह दिखा सकते हैं?
	kya mujhe aap yah/vah dikha sakte hain?

YOU MAY SEE…

खुला/बंद	open/closed
लंच के लिए बंद	closed for lunch
फिटिंग कक्ष	fitting room
खजांची	cashier
केवल नकद	cash only
क्रेडिट कार्ड स्वीकार्य हैं।	credit cards accepted
व्यावसायिक	business hours
निकास	exit

That's not quite what I want.	यह वह नहीं है जो मैं चाहता / चाहती हूं
	*yah vah nahin hai jo main chahta **m** / chahti **f** hoon*
No, I don't like it.	नहीं, मुझे यह पसंद नहीं आता है।
	nahin mujhe yah pasand nahin aata hai
It's too expensive.	यह बहुत महंगा है। *yah bahut mahnga hai*
I have to think about it.	मुझे उसके बारे में सोचना पड़ेगा।
	mujhe uske bare main sochna padega
I'll take it.	मैं उसे ले जाऊंगा / जाऊंगी ।
	*main use le jaoonga **m** / jaoongi **f***

Paying & Bargaining

How much?	कितना? *kitna?*
I'll pay...	मैं...भुगतान करूंगा / करूंगी
	*main...bhugtan karoonga **m** / karoongi **f***
in cash	नकद में *nakad main*
by credit card	क्रेडिट कार्ड द्वारा *credit card ke dwara*
by traveler's cheque	यात्री चेक द्वारा *yaatri cheque dwara*
A receipt, please.	कृपया रसीद दें। *kripya rasid dein*
That's too much.	यह बहुत अधिक है। *yah bahut adhik hai*
I'll give you...	मैं आपको...दूंगा / दूंगी। *main aapko...doonga **m** / doongi **f***
I have only...rupee.	मेरे पास केवल...रुपये हैं। *mere paas keval...rupee hain*
Is that your best price?	क्या यह आपका सर्वोत्तम मूल्य है?
	kya yah aapka sarvaottam mulya hai?
Can you give me a discount?	क्या आप मुझे छूट दे सकते हैं?
	kya aap mujhe chhoot de sakte hain?

For Numbers, see page 165.

Remember, if making a payment in cash, only accept and exchange crisp, clean, untorn, unmarked bills.

YOU MAY HEAR...

आप कैसे भुगतान कर रहे हैं?
aap kaise bhugtaan kar rahe hain?

How are you paying?

आपका क्रेडिट कार्ड भुगतान विफल रहा है।
aapka credit card bhugtaan vifal raha hai

Your credit card has been declined.

कृपया, आईडी दें। *kripya, ID dein*

ID please.

हम क्रेडिट कार्ड स्वीकार नहीं करते हैं।
hum credit card swikaar nahin karte hain

We don't accept credit cards.

कृपया, केवल नकद दें। *kripya, keval nakad dein*

Cash only, please.

Making a Complaint

I'd like...	मैं...चाहता / चाहती हूं *main... chahta m / chahti f hoon*
to exchange this	इसे बदलना *ise badalana*
a refund	एक रीफंड *ek refund*
to see the manager	प्रबंधक से मिलना *prabandhak se milna*

Services

| Can you recommend...? | क्या आप...सुझा सकते हैं? *kya aap... sujha sakte hain?* |

a barber	एक नाई *ek naai*
a dry cleaner	एक ड्राईक्लीनर *ek dry cleaner*
a hairstylist	एक हेयरस्टाइलिस्ट *ek hairstylist*
a Laundromat	एक धोने की मशीन [लॉन्ड्रेट]
[launderette]	*ek dhone ki machine[launderette]*
a nail salon	एक नेल सैलोन *ek nail salon*
a spa	एक स्पा *ek spa*
a travel agency	एक ट्रैवल एजेंसी *ek travel agency*
Can you…this?	क्या आप इसे…कर सकते हैं?
	kya aap ise…kar sakte hain?
alter	ऑल्टर *alter*
clean	साफ *saaf*
fix	ठीक *thik*
press	प्रेस *press*
When will it be ready?	यह कब तक तैयार हो जाएगा?
	yah kab tak taiyaar ho jayega?

Hair & Beauty

I'd like…	मैं…चाहता / चाहती हूं *main…chahta **m** / chahta **f** hoon*
an appointment for	आज/कल के लिए मिलने का समय
today/tomorrow	*aaj/kal ke liye milne ka samaya*
some color/	कुछ कलर/हाईलाइट्स
highlights	*kuch color/ highlights*
my hair styled/	मेरे स्टाइल्ड/ब्लो-ड्राइड बाल
blow-dried	*mere styled/blow-dried baal*
a haircut	एक हेयरकट *ek haircut*
an eyebrow/	एक आइब्रो/बिकिनी वैक्स
bikini wax	*ek eyebrow/bikini wax*
a facial	एक फेशियल *ek facial*
some henna	कुछ हिना *kuch henna*
a manicure/	एक मैनीक्योर/पेडिक्योर *ek manicure/ pedicure*
pedicure	

a (sports) massage	एक (स्पोर्ट्स) मसाज	*ek (sports) massage*
A trim, please.	कृपया, एक ट्रिम	*kripya, ek trim*
Not too short.	बहुत छोटा नहीं।	*bahut chota nahin*
Shorter here.	यहां से छोटा	*yahan se chota*
Do you offer…?	क्या आप…ऑफर करते हैं?	*kyaa aap…offer karte hain?*
acupuncture	एक्यूपंक्चर	*acupuncture*
aromatherapy	एरोमाथिरेपी	*aromatherapy*
oxygen	ऑक्सीजन	*oxygen*
a sauna	एक सौना	*ek sauna*

Antiques

How old is it?	यह कितना पुराना है?	*yah kitna purana hai?*
Do you have anything from the…period?	क्या आपके पास…अवधि की कोई चीज है?	*kya aapke paas…awadhi ki koi cheez hai?*
Do I have to fill out any forms?	क्या मुझे कोई फॉर्म भरना है?	*kya mujhe koi form bharna hai?*
Is there a certificate of authenticity?	क्या कोई विश्वसनीयता का प्रमाण पत्र है?	*kya koi vishwasniyata praman patra hai?*
Can you ship/ wrap it?	क्या आप इसे भेज/लपेट सकते हैं?	*kya aap ise bhej/lapet sakte hain?*

Clothing

I'd like...	मैं...चाहता/चाहती हूं *main...chahta/chahti hoon*
Can I try this on?	क्या मैं इसे आजमा सकता / सकती हूं?
	*kya main ise aajma sakta **m** / sakti **f** hoon?*
It doesn't fit.	यह फिट नहीं बैठता है। *yah fit nahin baithta hai*
It's too...	यह बहुत...है। *yah bahut hai*
big/small	बड़ा/छोटा *bada chota*
short/long	छोटा/लंबा *chota/lamba*
tight/loose	कसा/ढीला *kasa/dheela*
Do you have this	क्या आपके पास यह...आकार में है?
in size...?	*kya aapke paas yah...aakar main hai?*
Do you have this in	क्या आपके पास यह और बड़े/छोटे आकार में है?
a bigger/smaller size?	*kya aapke paas yah aur bade/chote aakar main hai?*

For Numbers, see page 165.

YOU MAY HEAR...

यह तुम पर बहुत अच्छा लगता है।
yah tum par achcha lagta hai

यह कैसे फिट होता है? *yah kaise fit hota hai?*

हमारे पास आपके आकार का नहीं है।
hamare paas aapke aakar ka nahin hai

That looks great on you.

How does it fit?
We don't have your size.

YOU MAY SEE...

पुरुष	men's
महिला	women's
बच्चे	children's

Colors

I'd like something…	मैं कुछ...चाहता / चाहती हूं
	*main kuch…chahta **m** / chahti **f** hoon*
beige	मटमैला *matmaila*
black	काला *kala*
blue	नीला *neela*
brown	भूरा *bhura*
green	हरा *hara*
gray	सिलेटी *sileti*
orange	नारंगी *narangi*
pink	गुलाबी *gulabi*
purple	बैंगनी *baingani*
red	लाल *laal*
white	सफेद *safed*
yellow	पीला *peela*

Clothes & Accessories

a backpack	एक बैकपैक *ek backpack*
a belt	एक बेल्ट *ek belt*
a bikini	एक बिकनी *ek bikini*
a blouse	एक ब्लाउज *ek blouse*

a bra	एक ब्रा *ek bra*
briefs [underpants]	अंतर्वस्त्र *anturvastra*
panties (ladie's)	जांघिया *jaanghiyaa*
a coat	एक कोट *ek coat*
a dress	एक ड्रेस *ek dress*
a hat	एक हैट *ek hat*
a jacket	एक जैकेट *ek jacket*
jeans	जींस *jeans*
pyjamas	पैजामा *pyjama*
pants [trousers]	पैंट *pant*
pantyhose [tights]	पैंटीहोस
a purse [handbag]	एक पर्स *ek purse [handbag]*
a raincoat	एक रेनकोट *ek raincoat*
a scarf	एक स्कार्फ *ek scarf*
a shirt	एक शर्ट *ek shirt*
shorts	शॉर्ट *short*
a skirt	एक स्कर्ट *ek skirt*
socks	मोजे *moje*
a suit	एक सूट मा *suit*
sunglasses	चश्मे *chasme*
a sweater	एक स्वेटर *ek sweater*
a sweatshirt	एक स्वेटशर्ट मा *sweatshirt*
a swimsuit	एक स्विमसूट *ek swimsuit*
a T-shirt	एक टी-शर्ट *ek T-shirt*

Textiles are ubiquitous, from the traditional **khadi** (homespun cotton) championed by Ghandi to the brilliantly colored mirrorwork Rajasthani fabrics and sumptuous Mysore and Varanasi silks. Traditional **saris** and **shalwar kameez** come in all colors, shapes and sizes.

a tie	एक टाई *ek tie*
underwear	अंडरवियर *underwear*

Fabric

I'd like...	मैं... चाहता / चाहती हूं *main chahta **m** / chahti **f** hoon*
cotton	कॉटन *cotton*
denim	डेनिम *denim*
lace	लेस *lace*
leather	चमड़ा *chamda*
linen	लिनेन *linen*
silk	सिल्क *silk*
wool	ऊन *oon*
Is it machine washable?	क्या यह मशीन में धोने योग्य है? *kya yah machine main dhone yogya hai?*

Shoes

I'd like...	मैं... चाहता / चाहती हूं *main chahta **m** / chahti **f** hoon*
high-heels/flats	ऊंची-हील/ फ्लैट *oonchi-heel/flat*
boots	बूट *boot*
loafers	लोफर *loafer*
sandals	सैंडल *sandal*

shoes	जूते *joote*
slippers	स्लिपर *slipper*
sneakers	स्निकर्स *sneakers*
Size...	आकार... *aakar...*

For Numbers, see page 165.

Sizes

small (S)	छोटा *(S) chota*
medium (M)	मध्यम *(M) madhyam*
large (L)	बड़ा *(L) bada*
extra large (XL)	अतिरिक्त बड़ा *atirikt bada (XL)*
petite	पतला *patla*
plus size	प्लस आकार *plus aakar*

Newsagent & Tobacconist

Do you sell English-language newspapers?	क्या आप अंग्रेज़ी- भाषा के सामाचार-पत्र बेचते हैं? *kya aap angrezi-bhasha ke samachar patra bechte hain?*
I'd like...	मैं... चाहता / चाहती हूं *main chahta **m** / chahti **f** hoon*
candy [sweets]	कैंडी *candy [sweets]*
chewing gum	च्यूइंग गम *chewing gum*
a chocolate bar	एक चॉकलेट बार *ek chocolate bar*
a cigar	एक सिगार *ek cigar*

a pack/carton of cigarettes	एक पैक/सिगरेट का कारटन	*ek pack/cigarettes ka carton*
a lighter	एक लाइटर	*ek lighter*
a magazine	एक मैगजीन	*ek magazine*
matches	माचिस	*matches*
a newspaper	एक समाचार-पत्र	*ek samachar-patra*
a pen	एक पेन	*ek pen*
a postcard	एक पोस्टकार्ड	*ek postcard*
a road/town map of......	का एक सड़क/शहर मानचित्र	*...ka ek sadak/shahar maanchitra*
stamps	डाक टिकट	*dak ticket*

127

Popular English-language newspapers include the *Times of India* (www.timesofindia.indiatimes.com), the *Indian Express* (**www.indianexpress.com**), *The Hindu* (**www.hinduonline.com**) and the *Hindustan Times* (**www.hindustantimes.com**).

Photography

I'd like...camera.	मैं...कैमरा पसंद करता / करती हूं!	*main... camera pasand karta **m** / karti **f** hoon.*
an automatic	एक स्वचालित	*ek swachalit*
a digital	एक डिजिटल	*ek digital*
a disposable	एक डिस्पोसेबल	*ek disposable*
I'd like...	मैं...चाहता / चाहती हूं	*main...chahta **m** / chahti **f** hoon*

a battery	एक बैटरी *ek battery*
digital prints	डिजिटल प्रिंट *digital print*
a memory card	एक मेमोरी कार्ड *ek memory card*
Can I print digital photos here?	क्या मैं यहां डिजिटल फोटो प्रिंट कर सकता / सकती हूं?
	*kya main yahan se digital photo print kar sakta **m** / sakti **f** hoon*

Souvenirs

a bottle of wine	शराब की एक बोतल *sharab ki ek bottle*
a box of chocolates	चॉकलेट का एक डिब्बा *chocolate ka ek dibba*
some crystal	कुछ क्रिस्टल *kuch crystal*
a doll	एक गुड़िया *ek gudia*
some jewelry	कुछ आभूषण *kuch aabhushan*
a key ring	एक चाबी का गुच्छा *ek chabi ka guchcha*
a postcard	एक पोस्टकार्ड *ek postcard*
some pottery	कुछ मिट्टी के बर्तन *kuch mitti ke bartan*
a T-shirt	एक टी-शर्ट *ek T-shirt*
a toy	एक खिलौना *ek khilauna*
Can I see this/that?	क्या मैं यह/उसे देख सकता / सकती हूं?
	*kya main yah/use dekh sakta **m** / sakti **f** hoon?*
I'd like…	मैं…चाहूंगा / चाहूंगी।
	*main chahoonga **m** / chahoongi **f***
a battery	एक बैटरी *ek battery*
a bracelet	एक ब्रेसलेट *ek bracelet*
a brooch	एक ब्रोच *ek brooch*
a clock	एक दीवार घड़ी *ek deewar ghadi*
earrings	कान की बालियां *kaan ki baaliyaan*
a necklace	एक गले का हार *ek gale ka haar*
a ring	एक अंगूठी *ek anguthi*
a watch	एक घड़ी *ek ghadi*

I'd like…	मैं… चाहूंगा / चाहूंगी
	main chahoonga **m** / *chahoongi* **f**
copper	तांबा *taamba*
crystal	क्रिस्टल *crystal*
diamonds	हीरे *hira*
white/yellow gold	सफेद/पीला सोना *safed/peela sona*
pearls	मोती *moti*
pewter	कांसा *kaansa*
platinum	प्लेटिनम *platinum*
sterling silver	स्टर्लिंग चांदी *sterling chaandi*
Is this real?	क्या यह असली है? *kya yah asli hai?*
Can you engrave it?	क्या आप इसे गोद सकते हैं?
	kya aap ise god sakte hain?

Traditional silk and wool carpets, colorful **dhurries** (the Indian version of the kilim) are made in many parts of the country. Gold, silver and jewellery, gems, metalware, carved figures, pottery and lacquerware and cane and leather goods can all be found in the shops and bazaars throughout India.

Sport & Leisure

ESSENTIAL

When's the game?	खेल कब है?	*khel kab hai?*
Where's...?	...कहां है?	*...kahan hai?*
the beach	तट	*tat*
the park	पार्क	*park*
the pool	पूल	*pool*
Is it safe to swim here?	क्या यहां तैरना सुरक्षित है?	
	kya yahan tairna surakshit hai?	
Can I hire clubs?	क्या मैं किराए पर क्लब ले सकता / सकती हूं?	
	kya main kiraye par club le sakta m / sakti f hoon?	
How much per hour/day?	प्रति घंटे/दिन कितना?	
	prarti ghante/din kitna?	
How far is it to...?	...के लिए कितना?	*...ke liye kitna?*
Show me on the map, please.	कृपया मानचित्र पर दिखाएं।	
	kripya maanchitra par dikhayein	

Watching Sport

When's...(game/race/tournament)?	...(खेल/रेस/टूर्नामेंट) कब है?	
	(khel/race/tournament) kab hai?	
the boxing	बॉक्सिंग	*boxing*
the cricket	क्रिकेट	*cricket*
the cycling	साइकिलिंग	*cycling*
the golf	गोल्फ	*golf*
the soccer [football]	फुटबॉल	*football*
the tennis	टेनिस	*tennis*

the volleyball	वॉलीबॉल *volleyball*
Who's playing?	कौन खेल रहा है? *kaun khel raha hai?*
Where's the racetrack/ stadium?	रेसट्रैक /स्टेडियम कहां है? *racetrack/stadium kahan hai?*
Where can I place a bet?	मैं कहां शर्त लगा सकता / सकती हूं? *main shart laga sakta **m** / sakti **f** hoon?*

For Tickets, see page 19.

Cricket is by far the most popular sport in India, with football a close second.

Playing Sport

Where is/are…?	….कहां है? *…kahan hai?*
the golf course	गोल्फ कोर्स *golf course*
the gym	जिम *gym*
the park	पार्क *park*
the tennis courts	टेनिस कोर्ट *tennis court*

How much per...	कितना प्रति... *kitna prati...*
day	दिन *din*
hour	घंटे *ghante*
game	खेल *khel*
round	चक्र *chakra*
Can I rent [hire]...?	क्या मैं...किराये पर ले सकता / सकती हूं?
	*kya main...kiraye par le sakta **m** / sakti **f** hoon?*
some clubs	कुछ क्लब *kuch club*
some equipment	कुछ उपकरण *kuch upkaran*
a racket	एक रैकेट *ek racket*

At the Beach/Pool

Where's the beach/pool?	तट/पूल कहां है? *tat/pool kahan hai?*
Is there a...?	क्या कोई...है? *kya koi...hai?*
kiddie pool	किडी पूल *kiddie pool*
indoor/ outdoor pool	इनडोर/आउटडोर पूल *indoor/outdoor pool*
lifeguard	जीवनसुरक्षा *jivansuraksha*
Is it safe...?	क्या...सुरक्षित है? *kya...surakshit hai?*
to swim	तैरना *tairna*

to dive	गोता लगाना	*gota lagana*
for children	बच्चों के लिए	*bachchon ke liye*
I'd like to hire…	मैं…किराये पर लेना चाहता / चाहती हूं	
	main kiraye par lena chahta m / chahti f hoon	
a deck chair	एक डेक कुर्सी	*ek deck kursi*
diving equipment	गोता लगाने का उपकरण	
	gota lagane ka upkaran	
a jet ski	एक जेट स्की	*ek jet ski*
a motorboat	एक मोटरबोट	*ek motorboat*
a rowboat	एक रोबोट	*ek robot*
snorkeling	स्नॉर्कलिंग उपकरण	
equipment	*snorkelling upkaran*	
a surfboard	एक सर्फबोर्ड	*ek surfboard*
a towel	एक तौलिया	*ek tauliya*
an umbrella	एक छाता	*ek chhata*
water skis	वॉटर स्की	*water skis*
a windsurfing board	एक विंडसर्फिंग बोर्ड	*ek windsurfing board*
For…hours.	…घंटों के लिए	
	…ghanton ke liye	

Out in the Country

A map of..., please.	कृपया,...का एक मानचित्र	
	kripya,...ka ek maanchitra	
this region	इस क्षेत्र	*is kshetra*
the walking routes	पैदल मार्ग	*paidal marg*
the bike routes	बाइक मार्ग	*bike marg*
the trails	ट्रेल	*trail*
Is it...?	क्या यह...है?	
	kya yah...hai?	
easy	आसान	*aasan*
difficult	मुश्किल	*mushkil*
far	दूर	*door*
steep	खड़ा	*khada*
How far is it to...?	यह...के लिए कितना दूर है?	
	yah...ke liye kitna door hai?	
I'm lost.	मैं खो गया	*main kho gaya*
Where's...?	...कहां है?	
	...kahan hai?	
the bridge	पुल	*pul*
the cave	गुफा	*gufaa*
the desert	रेगिस्तान	*registaan*
the farm	खेत	*khet*
the field	खलिहान	*khalihaan*
the forest	वन	*van*
the hill	पहाड़	*pahad*
the lake	झील	*jheel*
the mountain	पर्वत	*parvat*
the nature preserve	प्राकृतिक संरक्षण	
	prakritk sanrakshan	
the national park	राष्ट्रीय उद्यान	
	rashtriya udyan	

the viewpoint	व्यूपॉइंट *viewpoint*
the park	पार्क *park*
the path	रास्ता *raasta*
the peak	शिखर *shikhar*
the picnic area	पिकनिक क्षेत्र *picnic kshetra*
the pond	तालाब *talab*
the river	नदी *nadi*
he safari park	सफारी पार्क *safari park*
the sea	सागर *sagar*
the tiger reserve	बाघ अभयारण्य *bagh abhyaranya*
the valley	घाटी *ghati*
the waterfall	झरना *jharna*

Going Out

ESSENTIAL

What's there to do at night?	रात में करने को क्या है? *raat mein karne ko kya hai?*
Do you have a program of events?	क्या तुम्हारे पास ईवेंटों का कार्यक्रम है? *kya tumhare paas eventon ka karyakram hai?*
What's playing tonight?	आज रात क्या खेल रहे हो? *aaj raat kya khel rahe ho?*
Where's...?	...कहां है? *...kahan hai?*
the downtown area	शहर *shahar*
the bar	बार *bar*
the dance club	डांस क्लब *dance club*

Entertainment

Can you recommend...?	क्या आप... सुझा सकते हैं? *kya aap sujha sakte hain?*
a concert	एक कॉन्सर्ट *ek concert*
a movie	एक मूवी *ek movie*
an opera	एक ओपेरा *ek opera*
a play	एक नाटक *ek natak*
When does it start/end?	यह कब शुरू/समाप्त होता है? *yah kab shuru/samapt hota hai?*
What's the dress code?	ड्रेस कोड क्या है? *dress code kya hai?*
I like...	मैं...पसंद करता / करती हूं *main...pasand karta **m** / karti **f** hoon*
classical music	शास्त्रीय संगीत *shashtriya sangit*
folk music	लोक संगीत *lok sangit*

jazz	जैज़ *jazz*
pop music	पॉप संगीत *pop sangit*
rap	रैप *rap*

For Tickets, see page 19.

Most cinemas in India show Bollywood films, although in larger cities, you will also find several screening Hollywood releases. Tamil language films (Kollywood) are popular in the south and Telugu Tollywood films are made in Hyderabad. The most popular music is film song, **filmi git**. This can be heard almost everywhere, from shops and the backs of rickshaws to temples.

YOU MAY HEAR...

कृपया , अपने मोबाइल [सेल] फोन बंद कर दें।
kripya, apne mobile [cell] phone band kar dein

Turn off your cell [mobile] phones, please.

Nightlife

What's there to do at night?	रात में करने को क्या है?
	raat main karne ko kya hai?
Can you recommend...?	क्या आप...सुझा सकते हैं?
	kya aap sujha sakte hain?
a bar	एक बार *ek bar*
a cabaret	एक कैबरे *ek cabaret*
a casino	एक कैसिनो *ek casino*
a dance club	एक डांस क्लब *ek dance club*
a gay club	एक गे क्लब *ek gay club*
a jazz club	एक जैज क्लब *ek jazz club*
a club with traditional music	पारंपरिक संगीत वाला एक क्लब
	paramparik sangit wala ek club
Is there live music?	क्या कोई लाइव संगीत है?
	kya koi live sangit hai?
How do I get there?	मैं वहां कैसे जा सकता / सकती हूं?
	main wahan kaise jaa sakta m / sakti f hoon?
Is there a cover charge?	क्या कोई कवर प्रभार है?
	kya koi cover prabhar hai?

Undoubtedly the best cities in India for partying are Mumbai and Goa. However, as more Western lifestyles are increasingly being adopted, other large cities are beginning to follow suit. Most bars and clubs will be located in the bigger, luxury hotels, all of which have strict admission policies. Lone female travelers be warned though, bars are still largely a male preserve and may be intimidating.

Let's go dancing.	आओ डांस के लिए चलते हैं।
	aao dance ke liye chalte hain
Is this area safe at night?	क्या यह क्षेत्र रात के लिए सुरक्षित है?
	kya yah kshetra raat ke liye surakshit hai?

Special Requirements

Business Travel

ESSENTIAL

I'm here on business.	मैं यहां व्यवसाय पर हूं।	*main yahan vyavsaya par hoon*
Here's my card.	यहां मेरा कार्ड है।	*yahan mera card hai*
Can I have your card?	क्या मुझे आपका कार्ड मिल सकता है।	
	kya mujhe aapka card mil sakta hai?	
I have a meeting with...	मेरी...के साथ बैठक है।	*meri... ke saath baithak hai*
Where's...?	...कहां है?	*kahan hai?*
the business center	व्यवसाय केंद्र	*vyavsaya kendra*
the convention hall	कन्वेन्शन हॉल	*convention hall*
the meeting room	बैठक कक्ष	*baithak kaksha*

The traditional **namaskaram** greeting with joined hands has been largely replaced by the Western handshake. Many women however prefer not to shake hands with men so do not offer your hand to a woman until invited to do so first.

On Business

I'm here for...	मैं...के लिए यहां हूं	*main ...ke liye yahan hoon*
a seminar	एक सेमिनार	*ek seminar*
a conference	एक सम्मेलन	*ek sammelan*
a meeting	एक बैठक	*ek baithak*
My name is...	मेरा नाम...है	*mera naam...hai*
May I introduce my colleague...	क्या मैं अपने सहयोगी से मिलवा सकता / सकती हूं...	*kya main apne sahyogi se milwa sakta m / sakti f hoon*

I have a meeting/an appointment with. . .	मेरी...के साथ बैठक/मुलाकात है।
	meri. . . ke saath baithak/mulakat hai
I'm sorry I'm late.	मुझे क्षमा करें मुझे देरी हो गई।
	mujhe kshma karein mujhe deri ho gayi
I need an interpreter.	मुझे दुभाषिए की आवश्यकता है।
	mujhe dubhashiye ki aavashyakta hai
You can contact at the. . .Hotel.	आप मुझसे...होटल में संपर्क कर सकते हैं ।
	aap mujhse. . .hotel mein sampark kar sakte hain
I'm here until. . .	मैं...तक यहां हूं *main. . . tak yahan hoon*
I need to. . .	मुझे...की आवश्यकता है *mujhe. . . ki aavashyakta hai*
make a call	एक कॉल करने की *ek call karne ki*
make a photocopy	एक प्रतिलिपि करने की *ek pratilipi karne ki*
send an email	एक ईमेल भेजने की *ek email bhejne ki*
send a fax	एक फैक्स भेजने की *ek fax bhejne ki*
send a package (for next-day delivery)	एक पैकेज भेजने की (अगले दिन की डिलीवरी के लिए) *ek package bhejne ki (agle din ki delivery ke liye)*

It was a pleasure to meet you. आपसे मिलकर खुशी हुई। *aapse milkar khusi hui*

For Communications, see page 48.

YOU MAY HEAR...

क्या आपके पास मिलने का समय है?	Do you have an
kya aapke paas milne ka samay hai?	appointment?
किसके साथ? *kiske saath?*	With whom?
वह बैठक में हैं। *wah baithak mein hain*	He/She is in a meeting.
कृपया, थोड़ा ठहरें *kripya thoda thahrein*	One moment, please.
सीट ग्रहण करें। *seat grahan karein*	Have a seat.
क्या आप कुछ पीना पसंद करेंगे?	Would you like something
kya aap kuch peena pasand karenge?	to drink?
आने के लिए धन्यवाद। *aane ke liye dhanyavad*	Thank you for coming.

Traveling with Children

ESSENTIAL

Is there a discount for kids?	क्या बच्चों के लिए कोई छूट है?
	kya bachchon ke liye koi chhoot hai?
Can you recommend a babysitter?	क्या आप किसी बेबीसिटर को सुझा सकते हैं?
	kya aap kisi babysitter ko sujha sakte hain?
Do you have a child's seat/highchair?	क्या आपके पास बच्चे की सीट/ ऊंची कुर्सी है?
	kya aapke paas bachche ki seat/unchi kursi hai?
Where can I change the baby?	मैं शिशु के कपड़े कहां बदल सकती हूं?
	main shishu ke kapde kahan badal sakti hoon?

Out & About

Can you recommend something for kids?	क्या आप बच्चों के लिए कुछ सुझा सकते हैं।
	kya aap bachchon ke liye kuch sujha sakte hain?
Where's...? ...	कहां है? ...kahan hai...?
the amusement park	एम्यूजमेंट पार्क *amusement park*
the arcade	आरकेड *arcade*
the kiddie [paddling] pool	किडी [पैडलिंग] पूल
	kiddie [paddling] pool
the park	पार्क *park*
the playground	खेल का मैदान *khel ka maidaan*
the zoo	चिड़ियाघर *chidiyaghar*
Are kids allowed?	क्या बच्चों को अनुमति है? *kya bachchon ko anumati hai?*
Is it safe for kids?	क्या यह बच्चों के लिए सुरक्षित है?
	kya yah bachchon ke liye surakshit hai?
Is it suitable for... year olds?	क्या यह...साल के बच्चों के लिए उपयुक्त है?
	kya yah...saal ke bacchhon ke liye upyukta hai?

For Numbers, see page 165.

YOU MAY HEAR...

कितना सुंदर! *Kitna sundar!*
इसका क्या नाम है? *iska kya naam hai?*
इसकी उम्र कितनी है? *iski kitni umra hai?*

How cute!
What's his/her name?
How old is he/she?

Baby Essentials

Do you have...?	क्या आपके पास...है?	*kya aapke paas...hai?*
a baby bottle	एक बेबी बोतल	*ek baby bottle*
baby food	शिशु आहार	*shishu aahar*
baby wipes	बेबी वाइप्स	*baby wipes*
a car seat	एक कार सीट	*ek car seat*
a children's menu /portion	बच्चों का मेन्यू/हिस्सा *bachchon ka menu/hissa*	
a child's seat/ highchair	बच्चे की सीट/ऊंची कुर्सी *bachche ki seat/unchi kursi*	
a crib/cot	पालना/खाट *palna/khat*	
diapers [nappies]	डायपर [नैपीज] *diaper [nappies]*	
formula	फार्मूला *formula*	
a pacifier [dummy]	एक पैसिफायर ख्डमी, *ek pacifier [dummy]*	
a playpen	एक प्लेपेन *ek playpen*	
a stroller [pushchair]	एक र.स्ट्रोलर [पुशचेयर] *ek stroller [pushchair]*	

Can I breastfeed the baby here?
क्या मैं शिशु को यहां दूध पिला सकती हूं?
kya main shishu ko yahan doodh pila sakti hoon?

Where can I breastfeed/change the baby?
मैं कहां शिशु को दूध पिला/उसके कपड़े बदल सकती हूं
main kahan shishu ko doodh pila/uske kapde badal sakti hoon?

For Dining with Children, see page 64.

Traveling with children in India is rewarding as so many of the sights and sounds will appeal to both adults and children. Factors to be aware of however include the hot and humid climate, unsafe drinking water (rehydration salts are vital), spicy food and the risk of rabies from bites from stray dogs and monkeys. Also, the disposal (and purchase) of diapers outside of the main cities will prove difficult due to an irregular refuse collection.

Babysitting

Can you recommend a babysitter?	क्या आप एक बेबीसिटर का सुझाव दे सकते हैं? *kya aap ek babysitter ka sujhav de sakte hain?*
How much do you/ they charge?	आप/वे इसकी कितनी कीमत लेंगे? *aap/ve iski kitni kimat lenge?*
I'll be back at...	मैं...तक वापस आऊंगा / आऊंगी *main...tak vapas aaoonga m / aaoongi f*
If you need to contact me, call...	यदि आप मुझसे संपर्क करना चाहते / चाहती हैं, तो...पर कॉल करें *yadi aap mujhse sampark karna chahte m / chahti f hain to... par call karein*

For Time, see page 167.

Health & Emergency

Can you recommend a pediatrician?	क्या आप किसी बाल रोग चिकित्सक को सुझा सकते हैं? *ya aap kisi baal rog chikitsak ko sujha sakte hain?*
My child is allergic to...	मेरे बच्चे को...से एलर्जी हो गई है। *mere bachche ko...allergy ho gayi hai*
My child is missing.	मेरा बच्चा लापता है। *mera bachcha lapata hai*
Have you seen a boy/girl?	क्या आपने किसी लड़के/लड़की को देखा है? *kya aapne kisi ladke/ladki ko dekha hai?*

For Police, see page 150.

Disabled Travelers

ESSENTIAL

Is there...?	क्या वहां...है?	*kya yahan...hai?*
access for the disabled	विकलांगों के लिए पहुंच	*viklango ke liye pahunch*
a wheelchair ramp	एक व्हीलचेयर रैंप	*ek wheelchair ramp*
a disabled-accessible toilet	विकलांग-अनुकूल शौचालय	*iklang-anukool shauchalaya*
I need...	मुझे...की आवश्यकता है।	*mujhe...ki aavashyakta hai*
assistance	सहायता	*sahaayata*
an elevator [a lift]	एक एलीवेटर [एक लिफ्ट]	*ek elevator [ek lift]*
a ground-floor room	भूतल पर एक कक्ष	*bhootal par ek kaksha*

Provisions for wheelchairs are generally poor in India, with poor roads and high kerbs, a lack of adapted toilets. However, locals tend to be extremely accommodating and helpful.

Asking for Assistance

I'm...	मैं...हूं	*main hoon*
disabled	विकलांग	*viklang*
visually impaired	नेत्रहीन	*netraheen*
deaf	बहरा	*bahra*
hearing impaired	सुनने की समस्या से पीड़ित	*sunane ki samsya se pidit*

unable to walk far/ use the stairs	दूर तक चलने/सीढ़ियों का उपयोग करने में असमर्थ *door tak chalne/sidhiyon ka upyog karne mein asamarth*
Please speak louder.	कृपया तेज बोलें *kripya tez bolein*
Can I bring my wheelchair?	क्या मैं अपनी व्हीलचेयर ला सकता / सकती हूं? *kya main wheelchair laa sakta m / sakti f hoon?*
Are guide dogs permitted?	क्या गाइड कुत्तों को अनुमति है? *kya guide kutton ko anumati hai?*
Can you help me?	क्या आप मेरी सहायता कर सकते हैं? *kya aap meri sahayta kar sakte hain?*
Please open/hold the door.	कृपया दरवाजा खोलें/पकड़कर रखें। *kripya darwaza kholein/pakadkar rakhein*

In an Emergency

Emergencies

ESSENTIAL

Help!	सहायता! *Sahayta*
Go away!	दूर चले जाओ! *Door chale jao*
Stop, thief!	रुको, चोर! *Ruko chor*
Get a doctor!	डॉक्टर को बुलाओ! *doctor ko bulao*
Fire!	आग! *Aag*
I'm lost.	मैं भटक गया हूं *main bhatak gaya hoon*
Can you help me?	क्या आप मेरी सहायता कर सकते हैं ? *kya aap meri sahayta kar sakte hain ?*

In an emergency, dial **108**.
This is an India-wide generic number for all emergencies.
Otherwise, dial:
Police: 100
Fire: 101
Ambulance: 102

Police

ESSENTIAL

Call the police!	पुलिस को बुलाओ! *police ko bulao*
Where's the police station?	पुलिस थाना कहां है? *police thana kahan hai?*
There was an accident/attack.	वहां दुर्घटना हुई थी/हमला हुआ था। *wahan durghatna hui thi/hamla hua tha*
My child is missing.	मेरा बच्चा लापता है। *mera bachcha lapata hai*
I need…	मुझे…की आवश्यकता है *mujhe aavashyakta hai*
an interpreter	एक दुभाषिया *ek dubhashiya*
to make a phone call.	फोन कॉल करने के लिए। *phone call karne ke liye*
I'm innocent.	मैं निर्दोष हूं। *main nirdosh hoon*

YOU MAY HEAR…

इस फॉर्म को भरो। *is form ko bharo* — Fill out this form.

कृपया, आपकी आईडी। *kripya aapki ID* — Your ID, please.

कब/कहां यह हुआ? *kab/kahan yah hua?* — When/Where did it happen?

वह कैसा दिखता / दिखती है? *wah kaisa dikhta m / dikhti f hai?* — What does he/she look like?

Crime & Lost Property

I need to report…	मुझे रिपोर्ट करने की आवश्यकता है… *mujhe report karne ki aavashyakta hai*
a mugging	एक डकैती *ek dacoiti*
a rape	एक बलात्कार *ek balatkaar*
a theft	एक चोरी *ek chori*

I was mugged.	मेरे ऊपर डाका पड़ा था।	*mere upar daka pada tha*
I was robbed.	मुझे लूटा गया था।	*mujhe loota gaya tha*
I lost…	मैंने गंवाया…	*maine gavanya*
…was stolen.	…चुरा ली गई थी।	*chura ki gayi thi*
My backpack	मेरा बैग	*mera bag*
My bicycle	मेरी साइकिल	*meri cycle*
My camera	मेरा कैमरा	*mera camera*
My (hire) car	मेरी (किराये की) कार	*meri (kiraye ki) car*
My computer	मेरा कंप्यूटर	*mera computer*
My credit card	मेरा क्रेडिट कार्ड	*mera credit card*
My jewelry	मेरे आभूषण	*mere aabhushan*
My money	मेरा पैसा	*mera paisa*
My passport	मेरा पासपोर्ट	*mera passport*
My purse [handbag]	मेरा पर्स [हैंडबैग]	*mera purse [handbag]*
My traveler's cheques	मेरे यात्री चेक	*mere yaatri cheques*
My wallet	मेरा पर्स	*mera purse*
I need a police report.	मुझे पुलिस रिपोर्ट की आवश्यकता है।	*mujhe police report ki aavashyakta hai?*
Where is the British/ American/Irish embassy?	ब्रिटेन/अमेरिका/आयरलैंड दूतावास कहां है?	*Britain/America/Ireland dootawas kahan hai?*

Health

ESSENTIAL

I'm sick.	मैं बीमार हूं। *main beemar hoon*
I need an English-speaking doctor.	मुझे अंग्रेजी-बोलने वाले डॉक्टर की आवश्यकता है। *mujhe angrezi-bolne wale docto ki aavashyakta hai*
It hurts here.	यह यहां दुखता है। *yah yahan dukhta hai*

Finding a Doctor

Can you recommend a doctor/dentist?	क्या आप किसी डॉक्टर/दंतचिकित्सक की सलाह दे सकते हैं? *kya aap kisi doctor/dantchikitsak ki salah de sakte hain?*
Can the doctor come here?	क्या डॉक्टर यहां आ सकता है? *kya doctor yahan aa sakta hai?*
I need an English-speaking doctor.	मुझे अंग्रेजी बोलने वाले डॉक्टर की आवश्यकता है। *mujhe angrezi bolne wale doctor ki aavashyakta hai*
What are the office hours?	कार्यालय के घंटे क्या हैं? *kaaryaalaya ke ghante kya hain?*
I'd like appointment for...	मुझे...के लिए मिलने का समय चाहिए *mujhe...ke liye milne ka samaya chahiye*
today	आज *aaj*
tomorrow	कल *kal*
as soon as possible	जल्द से जल्द *jald se jald*
It's urgent.	यह अत्यावश्यक है। *yah atyaavashyak hai*

Symptoms

I'm bleeding.	मेरा खून बह रहा है। *mera khoon baha raha hai*
I'm constipated.	मुझे कब्ज है। *mujhe kabz hai*
I'm dizzy.	मुझे चक्कर आ रहा है। *mujhe chakkar aa raha hai*

I'm nauseous.	मुझे मिचली आ रही है। *mujhe michli aa rahi hai*
I'm vomiting.	मैं उल्टी कर रहा हूं। *main ulti kar raha hoon*
It hurts here.	यह यहां दुखता है। *yah yahan dukhta hai*
I have…	मुझे है… *mujhe hai*
an allergic reaction	एक एलर्जी की प्रतिक्रिया *ek allergy ki pratikriya*
chest pain	छाती में दर्द *chati main dard*
cramps	जकड़न *jakdan*
diarrhea	डायरिया *diarrhea*
an earache	कान में दर्द *kaan main dard*
a fever	बुखार *bukhaar*
pain	पीड़ा *peeda*
a rash	एक खरोंच *ek kharonch*
a sprain	मोच *moch*
some swelling	कुछ सूजन *kuch soojan*
a sore throat	कंठव्रण *kanthvran*
a stomach ache	पेट में दर्द *pet main dard*
I've been sick for…days.	मैं…दिनों से बीमार हूं। *main…dinon se beemar hoon*

For Numbers, see page 165.

Conditions

I'm...	मैं...हूं *main...hoon*
anemic	अनीमिया पीड़ित
	aemia peedit hoon
asthmatic	दमा पीड़ित
	dama peedit hoon
diabetic	मधुमेह पीड़ित
	madhumeh peedit hoon
I'm epileptic.	मिर्गी पीड़ित
	mirgi peedit hoon
I'm allergic to antibiotics/penicillin.	मुझे एंटीबायोटिक्स/पेनिसिलिन से एलर्जी है। *mujhe antibiotic/penicillin se allergy hai*
I have...	मुझे...है *mujhe...hai*
arthritis	आर्थराइटिस
	arthiritis
a heart condition	दिल की बीमारी
	dil ki beemari
high/low blood pressure	उच्च/निम्न रक्तचाप
	uccha/nimna raktachap
I'm on...	मैं...पर हूं *main...par hoon*

For Meals & Cooking, see page 67.

YOU MAY HEAR...

क्या गड़बड़ है? *kya gadbad hai?* — What's wrong?

यह कहां दुखता है? *yah kahan dukhta hai?* — Where does it hurt?

क्या यह यहां दुखता है? *kya yah yahan dukhta hai?* — Does it hurt here?

क्या आप दवाओं पर हैं? *kya aap dawaon par hain?* — Are you on medication?

क्या आपको किसी चीज से एलर्जी है ? *kya aapko kisi cheez se allergy hai?* — Are you allergic to anything?

अपना मुंह खोलें। *apna muh kholen* — Open your mouth.

गहरी सांस लें। *gahri saans lein* — Breathe deeply.

कृपया खांसें। *kripya khaanse* — Cough, please.

अस्पताल जाएं। *aspataal jaayen* — Go to the hospital.

Treatment

Do I need a prescription/medicine? — क्या मुझे नुस्खे/दवा की आवश्यकता है? *kya mujhe nuskhe/dawa ki aawashyakta hai?*

Can you prescribe a generic drug [unbranded medication]? — क्या आप जेनरिक दवा [बिना ब्रांड वाली दवा] सुझा सकते हैं? *kya aap generic dawa [bina brand wali dawa] sujha sakte hain?*

Where can I get it? — इसे मैं कहां पा सकता हूं? *ise main kahan paa sakta hoon?*

For What to Take, see page 158.

Hospital

Notify my family, please. — कृपया, मेरे परिवार को सूचित करें। *kripya mere parivaar ko suchit karein*

I'm in pain. — मैं पीड़ा में हूं। *main peeda main hoon*

I need a doctor/nurse. — मुझे डॉक्टर/नर्स की आवश्यकता है। *mujhe doctor/nurse ki aavashyakta hai*

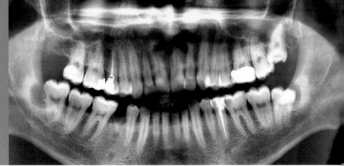

When are visiting hours?	मिलने का समय कब है? *milne ka samaya kab hai*
I'm visiting...	मैं मुलाकात कर रहा / रही हूं... *main mulakaat kar raha **m** / rahi **f** hoon*

Dentist

I have...	मेरा...है। *mera hai*
a broken tooth	एक टूटा हुआ दांत *ek toota hua daant*
a lost filling	एक गुम हुई फिलिंग *ek gum hui filling*
a toothache	दांत दर्द *daant dard*
Can you fix this denture?	क्या आप इन नकली दांतों को ठीक कर सकते हैं? *kya aap in nakli daanton ko thik kar sakte hain?*

Gynecologist

I have cramps/ a vaginal infection.	मुझे जकड़न/योनिक संक्रमण है। *mujhe jakdan/yonic sankraman hai?*
I missed my period.	मुझे मासिक धर्म नहीं हुआ। *mujhe masic dharma nahin hua*
I'm on the Pill.	मैं गोली पर हूं। *main goli par hoon*
I'm (...months) pregnant.	मैं (...महीनों) से गर्भवती हूं। *main (...mahinon) se garbhwati hoon*

I'm not pregnant.	मैं गर्भवती नहीं हूं। *main garbhwati nahin hoon*
My last period was...	मेरा अंतिम मासिक धर्म...था।
	mera antim masik dharma... tha

For Numbers, see page 165.

Optician

I lost...	मैंने...खो दिए *maine kho diye*
a contact lens	एक कॉन्टैक्ट लेंस *ek contact lens*
my glasses	मेरे चश्मे *mere chasme*
a lens	एक लेंस *ek lens*

Payment & Insurance

How much?	कितना? *kitna?*
Can I pay by credit card?	क्या मैं क्रेडिट कार्ड से भुगतान कर सकता हूं?
	kya main credit card se bhugtaan kar sakta hoon?
I have insurance.	मेरा बीमा है। *mera bema hai*
I need a receipt for my insurance.	मुझे अपने बीमा के लिए रसीद की आवश्यकता है।
	mujhe apne bema ke liye rasid ki aavashyakta hai

Pharmacy

ESSENTIAL

Where's the pharmacy?	दवा की दुकान कहां है?	*dawa ki dukan kahan hai?*
What time does it open/close?	यह किस समय खुलती/बंद होती है?	
	yah kis samaya khulti/band hoti hai?	
What would you recommend for...?	आप...के लिए क्या सुझाव देंगे?	
	aap...ke liye kya sujhav denge?	
How much do I take?	मुझे कितना लेना है?	*mujhe kitna lena hai?*
I'm allergic to...	मुझे...से एलर्जी है।	*mujhe...se allergy hai*

What to Take

How much do I take?	मुझे कितना लेना है?	
	mujhe kitna lena hai?	
How often?	कितनी बार?	*kitni baar?*
Is it safe for children?	क्या यह बच्चों के लिए सुरक्षित है?	
	kya yah bachchon ke liye surakshit hai?	
I'm taking...	मैं...ले रहा/रही हूं	*main...le raha/rahi hoon*
Are there side effects?	क्या दुष्प्रभाव हैं?	*kya dushprabhav hain?*
I need something for...	मुझे...के लिए कुछ चाहिए	
	mujhe...ke liye kuchh chahiye	
a cold	सर्दी-जुकाम	*sardi-jukhaam*
a cough	खांसी	*khasin*
diarrhea	डायरिया	*diarrhea*
a headache	सिरदर्द	*sirdard*
insect bites	कीड़े का काटा	*keede ka kaata*
motion sickness	दस्त की बीमारी	*dast ki bemari*
a sore throat	कंठव्रण	*kanthvran*

sunburn	सनबर्न *sunburn*
a toothache	दांतदर्द *daantdard*
an upset stomach	पेट की खराबी *pet ki kharabi*

YOU MAY SEE…

दिन में एक/तीन बार	once/three times a day
गोली	tablets
ड्रॉप	drop
चम्मच	teaspoon
…आहार	…meals
बाद	after
पहले	before
साथ	with
खाली पेट	on an empty stomach
पूरा खाली	swallow whole
उनींदापन कर सकता है	may cause drowsiness
निगला नहीं जाता है	do not ingest

Basic Supplies

I'd like...	मैं...चाहूंगा / चाहूंगी। *main chahoonga **m** /chahoongi **f***
acetaminophen [paracetamol]	एसिटामिनोफेन [पेरासीटामॉल] *acetaminophen [paracetamol]*
antiseptic cream	एंटीसेप्टिक क्रीम *antiseptic cream*
aspirin	एस्प्रिन *aspirin*
Band-Aid [plasters]	बैंड-एड [प्लास्टर] *Band-Aid [plasters]*
bandages	बैंडेज *bandages*
a comb	एक कंघा *ek kangha*
condoms	कंडोम *condom*
contact lens solution	कॉन्टैक्ट लेंस सॉल्यूशन *contact lens solution*
deodorant	डियोड्रेंट *deodorant*
a hairbrush	एक कंघी *ek kanghi*
hairspray	हेयरस्प्रे *hairspray*
ibuprofen	आईब्यूप्रोफेन *ibuprofen*
insect repellent	कीटरोधी *keetrodhi*
lotion [moisturizing cream]	लोशन [मॉश्चराइजिंग क्रीम] *lotion [moisturizing cream]*
a nail file	नेल फाइल *nail file*
a (disposable) razor	एक (डिस्पोजेबल रेजर) *ek (disposable) razor*
razor blades	रेजर ब्लेड *razor blade*
sanitary napkins [pads]	सैनिटरी नैपकिन [पैड] *sanitary napkins [pads]*
scissors	कैंची *kainchi*

shampoo/ conditioner	शैंपू/कंडीशनर *shampoo/ conditioner*
soap	साबुन *saabun*
sunscreen	सनस्क्रीन *sunscreen*
tampons	टेंपोन *tampon*
tissues	टिश्यू *tissues*
toilet paper	टॉयलट पेपर *toilet paper*
toothpaste	टूथपेस्ट *toothpaste*

For Baby Essentials, see page 144.

The Basics

Grammar

Regular Verbs

मैं ह	main hoon	-	I am
हम हैं	ham hain	-	We are
तू ह	too hai	-	You are (Intimate)
आप हैं	aap hain	-	You are (Formal)
तुम हो	tum ho	-	You are (Casual)
यह है	yeh hai	-	He / She / This is (Near)
ये ह	ye hain	-	These / They are (Near)
वह है	voh hai	-	He / She / That is (Far)
वे हैं	ve hain	-	Those / They are (Far)

For example:
My name is मैं नीता हूं *main neetaa hoon* - I am Nita

Word Order

The typical word order of most sentences is:
subject object verb
Whereas in English it is subject, verb, object.

Note, in conversational Hindi, the subject can often be placed at the end of the sentence.

The Devangari script contains 10 vowels and 40 consonants and is characterized by bars on top of the symbols. Hindi is highly phonetic; i.e. words are pronounced as they are written.

Negations

To negate a sentence in Hindi you simply put नहीं *naheen* before the verb.
For example:

मैं लंबा नहीं हूं *main lambaa naheen hoon*	I am not tall.
आप लंबे नहीं हैं *aap lambe naheen hain*	You are not tall

Note that आप *aap* is treated as plural!

वह अंग्रेज नहीं है *vah Angrez nahin hai*	She is not English.

In fact in the negative you can even drop the auxiliary (that is the correct form of होना *Honaa* ie हूं *hoon*, है *hai*, etc).
For example:

हम गोश्त नहीं खाते *ham gosht naheen khaate*	We do not eat meat.

Nouns & Articles

Hindi nouns have no articles (i.e. **a**, **an** or **the**). All Hindi nouns are either masculine or feminine.

1. All masculine nouns that end in **a** change to **e** in the plural.
For example:

	Hindi (singular)	Hindi (plural)
Boy	लड़का *ladkaa*	लड़के *ladke*

2. All feminine nouns, except those ending in **i**, add **en** to form the plural.
For example:

Book	किताब *kitaab*	किताबें *kitaaben*

3. All feminine nouns ending in **i** take **yan** for plural. For example:

Girl	लड़की *ladki*	लड़कियां *ladkiyan*

Questions

Most straightforward sentences can easily be turned into a question by putting **kya** in front of the sentence and raising the pitch of the voice at the end of the sentence.

For example:

| धोबी है *Dhobi hai* | There is a washerman. |
| क्या धोबी है? *Kya dhobi hai?* | Is there a washerman? |

The key question words are as follows:

What is?	क्या है? *Kya hai?*
Where is?	कहां है? *Kahan hai?*
Why?	क्यों? *Kyun?*
Who is?	कौन है? *Kaun hai?*
When is?	कब है? *Kab hai?*
How?	कैसा? *Kaisa?*

Numbers

ESSENTIAL

0	शून्य	*shunya*
1	एक	*ek*
2	दो	*do*
3	तीन	*teen*
4	चार	*chaar*
5	पाँच	*paanch*
6	छह	*che*
7	सात	*saat*
8	आठ	*aath*
9	नौ	*nau*
10	दस	*dus*
11	ग्यारह	*gyarah*
12	बारह	*baarah*
13	तेरह	*teraah*
14	चौदह	*chaudaah*
15	पंद्रह	*pandrah*
16	सोलह	*solaah*
17	सत्रह	*satraah*
18	अठारह	*athaarah*
19	उन्नीस	*unnees*
20	बीस	*bees*
21	इक्कीस	*ikkis*
22	बाईस	*baaees*
30	तीस	*tees*
31	इकत्तीस	*ikuttees*
40	चालीस	*chaalees*

50	पचास *pachaas*
60	साठ *saath*
70	सत्तर *sutur*
80	अस्सी *ussi*
90	नब्बे *nubbe*
100	सौ *sau*
101	एक सौ एक *ek sau ek*
200	दो सौ *do sau*
500	पाँच सौ *panch sau*
1,000	एक हजार *ek hazaar*
10,000	दस हजार *dus hazaar*
100,000	एक लाख *ek laakh*
1,000,000	दस लाख *dus laakh*

Ordinal Numbers

first	प्रथम *pratham*
second	द्वितीय *dweeteeye*
third	तृतीय *triteeye*
fourth	चतुर्थ *chaturth*
fifth	पंचम *panchum*
once	एक बार *ek baar*
twice	दो बार *do baar*
three times	तीन बार *teen baar*

Time

ESSENTIAL

What time is it?	इस समय क्या बजा है?
	is samay kya baja hai
It's midday.	यह दोपहर है। *yah dophar hai*
At midnight.	आधी रात में। *aadhi raat mein*
From one o'clock to	एक बजे से दो बजे तक
two o'clock.	*ek baje se do do baje tak*
Five past three.	पांच बजकर तीन मिनट
	paanch bajkar teen minute
A quarter to ten.	दस बजकर पंद्रह मिनट
	dus bajkar pandrah minute
5:30 a.m./p.m.	5:30 सुबह/शाम *subah/sham*

Days

ESSENTIAL

Monday	सोमवार *somwaar*
Tuesday	मंगलवार *mangalwaar*
Wednesday	बुधवार *budhwaar*
Thursday	गुरुवार *guruwaar*
Friday	शुक्रवार *shukrwaar*
Saturday	शनिवार *shaniwaar*
Sunday	रविवार *raviwaar*

Dates

yesterday	गुजरा हुआ कल *gujraa hua kul*
today	आज *aaj*
tomorrow	आने वाला कल *aane waala kul*
day	दिन *din*
week	सप्ताह *saptah*
month	महीना *mahina*
year	साल *saal*
Happy birthday!	जन्मदिन मुबारक! *janamdin mubaarak!*
Happy New Year!	नया साल मुबारक! *naya saal mubaarak!*

Months

January	जनवरी *junwaree*
February	फरवरी *furwaree*
March	मार्च *march*
April	अप्रैल *aprail*
May	मई *mai*
June	जून *june*
July	जुलाई *july*
August	अगस्त *agast*
September	सितंबर *sitambar*
October	अक्तूबर *aktubar*
November	नवंबर *navambar*
December	दिसम्बर *disambar*

Seasons

spring	वसंत *vasant*	
summer	गर्मी *garmee*	
fall [autumn]	पतझड़ *patjhad*	
winter	जाड़ा *jaada*	

Holidays

January 21	ईद-उल-जुहा/ बकरीद	*Id-Ul-Juha/ Bakrid*
January 26	गणतंत्र दिवस	*Republic Day*
February 20	मुहर्रम	*Muharram*
March 8	महाशिवरात्रि	*Maha shivratri*
March 25	गुड फाइडे	*Good Friday*
March 26	होली	*Holi*
April 22	महावीर जयंती	*Mahavir Jayanti*
April 22	मिलाद-उन-नबी	*Milad-Un-Nabi (Birthday of Prophet Mohammed)*
May 23	बुद्ध पूर्णिमा	*Buddha Purnima*
August 15	स्वतंत्रता दिवस	*Independence Day*
October 02	महात्मा गांधी जयंती	*Mahatma Gandhi's Birthday*
October 11	महाअष्टमी	*Maha Ashtami*
October 12	दशहरा/ विजयादशमी	*Dussehra/ Vijay Dashmi*
November 01	दिवाली/दीपावली	*Diwali/Deepavali*

November 04	ईद-उल-फितर	*Eid-al-Fitr (Muslim Festival)*
November 15	गुरु नानक जयंती	*Guru Nanak's Birthday*
December 25	क्रिसमस	*Christmas*

* Most of these dates follow a lunar calendar and the dates move each year.

Diwali is India's biggest national celebration, the Festival of Lights commemorates the homecoming of Rama and Sita with the lighting of innumerable oil lamps and the setting-off of vast quantities of fireworks.

Conversion Tables

When you know	Multiply by	To find
ounces	28.3	grams
pounds	0.45	kilograms
inches	2.54	centimeters
feet	0.3	meters
miles	1.61	kilometers
square inches	6.45	sq. centimeters
square feet	0.09	sq. meters
square miles	2.59	sq. kilometers
pints (U.S./Brit)	0.47/0.56	liters
gallons (U.S./Brit)	3.8/4.5	liters
Fahrenheit	-32, / 1.8	Celsius
Celsius	+32 , x 1.8	Fahrenheit

Kilometers to Miles Conversions

1 km = 0.62 miles	**20 km** = 12.4 miles	
5 km = 3.1 miles	**50 km** = 31 miles	
10 km = 6.20 miles	**100 km** = 62 miles	

Measurement

1 gram	= **1000 milligrams**	= 0.035 oz.
1 kilogram (kg)	= **1000 grams**	= 2.2 lb
1 liter (l)	= **1000 milliliters**	= 1.06 U.S./0.88
1 centimeter	= **10 millimeters**	= 0.4 inch (cm)
1 meter (m)	= **100 centimeters**	= 39.37 inches/ 3.28 ft.
1 kilometer	= **1000 meters**	= 0.62 mile (km)

Temperature

-40°**C** = -40°F	**-1**°**C** = 30°F	**20**°**C** = 68°F
-30°**C** = -22°F	**0**°**C** = 32°F	**25**°**C** = 77°F
-20°**C** = -4°F	**5**°**C** = 41°F	**30**°**C** = 86°F
-10°**C** = 14°F	**10**°**C** = 50°F	**35**°**C** = 95°F
-5°**C** = 23°F	**15**°**C** = 59°F	

Oven Temperature

100° **C** = 212° F	**177**° **C** = 350° F
121° **C** = 250° F	**204**° **C** = 400° F
149° **C** = 300° F	**260**° **C** = 500° F

avkaash prapt hona

d, to be अवकाश khuda

return (adj.) वापसी waapsee

~ ticket वापसी टिकट
waapsee ticket

return, to वापस होना waapse
hona

reverse the charges, to उल्टा कर देना shulk
shulk ulta kar dena

revolting राजद्रोही raajdrohi

rheumatism गठिया guthiyaa

पसली puslee

चावल chaawal

(direction): on the ~ दाएं
ी और daanyan...

robb

loot

robbe

rock m

sangeer

rolls रौल्स

romantic

roof छत ch

~-rack रफ़

room कमरा

~ service रूम

rope रस्सी rassi

round गोलाई go

~ neck गोल गल

round (of golf) राउंड

round-trip वापसी

~ ticket वापसी
waapse

English – Hindi

Hindi Alphabet

		Ei	ए/ई
a	अ	Dha	ध/ढ
B	ब	Ma	म
L	ल	Tha	थ/ठ
Sa	स	Ai	ऐ
Aa	आ	Fa	फ
Bha	भ	Na	न
Li	लि	Tha	थ/ठ
Sha	ष	I	इ
E	ए	Fi	फि
Ca	क	N'a	न
Li	लि	T'ha	थ
Shha	श	O	ओ
Ii	ई	G	ग
Chha	छ	Nia	निया
Lii	ली	Thha	थ
Ta	ट/त	Oi	ओइ
Ei	ए/ई	Gha	घ
Da	द/ड	Nae	ने
Lii	ली	oii	ओई
T'a	त	Ghi	घी

Ni	नि
uu	उ
Ha	ह
Oms	ओम्स
Va	व
Ou	औ
Ja	ज
Pa	प
Ya	य
U	उ
Jha	झ
Qi	क्वि
Yi	यि
Ka	क
Ra	र
Za	ज
Kha	ख
Ri	ऋ
Khi	खि
Ri	रि

a few सिर्फ कुछ *sirf kuch*
a little थोड़ा *thodaa*
a lot बहुत *bahut*
a.m. पूर्वाह्न *purvahaan*
abbey मठ *muth*
about (approximately) लगभग
lugbhug
abroad विदेश में *videsh mein*
accept, to स्वीकार करना
sweekaar karnaa
access only केवल प्रवेश
kewal pravesh
accident (road) दुर्घटना
durghutnaa
accompany, to साथ देना
aath dena
acne मुहाँसा *muhaansaa*
acrylic ऐक्रिलिक *acrylic*
actor/actress अभिनेता/अभिनेत्री
abhineta/abhinetree
adapter एडेप्टर *adapter*
address पता *pata*
adjoining room आसन्न कमरा
aasun kumra
admission charge प्रवेश शुल्क
pravesh shulk
adult *(n)* बड़े *bade*
after (time) बाद में *baad mein*
after-shave आफ्टर शेव
after-shave
after-sun lotion
आफ्टर-सन लोशन
after-sun lotion

afternoon, in the दोपहर में
dopeher mein
aged: to be ~ उम्रदराज: उम्रदराज
होना *umerdaraaz : umerdaraaz hona*
ago पहले *pehle*
agree: I don't agree
सहमत होना: मैं सहमत नहीं
sehmat hona: main sehmat nahin
air: ~ conditioning
हवा: वातानुकूलित *hawa: vatanukulit;*
~ mattress हवा वाली गद्दी
hava waali gaddi;
~ pump हवा भरने वाला
hava bharne waala;
~ sickness bag
बीमारी वाली थैली
bimaari waali theli;
~ mail हवाई मेल *hawaai mail*
airport एयरपोर्ट *airport*
aisle seat गलियारे के पास वाली
सीट *galiyaari ke paas waali seat*
alarm clock अलार्म घड़ी
alarm ghadi
alcoholic (drink) ड्रिंक *drink*
all सब *sub*
allergic, to be एलर्जी होना
allergy hona
allergy एलर्जी *allergy*
allowance भत्ता *bhatta*
almost लगभग *lugbhug*
alone अकेला *akelaa*
already पहले से *pehle se*
also भी *bhi*

alter, to परिवर्तित करना
parvartit kurnaa
alumin(i)um foil
एल्युमिनीयम फॉयल
aluminium foil
always हमेशा *hameshaa*
a.m. पूर्वाह्न *purvahan*
am: I am हूँ: मैं हूँ
hoon: main hoon
amazing अद्भुत *adbhut*
ambassador राजदूत *raajdoot*
ambulance एंबुलेंस *ambulance*
American अमेरिकन *american*
amount राशि *raashi*
anaesthetic बेहोशी *behoshi*
and और *aur*
animal जानवर *jaanwar*
anorak टोपीदार बरसाती कोट
topidaar barsaati coat
another अन्य *anya*
antacid एंटासिड *antacid*
antibiotics
एंटीबायोटिक *antibiotic*
antifreeze एंटीफ्रीज
antifreeze
antique प्राचीन *pracheen*
~ **store** प्राचीन वस्तुओं की दुकान
pracheen vustuaon kee dukaan
antiseptic एंटीसेप्टिक *antiseptic*
~ **cream** एंटीसेप्टिक क्रीम
antiseptic cream
any कोई *koi*
anyone: ~ **else** कोई भी: कोई
और *koi bhi: koi aur*

does anyone speak English?
क्या कोई अंग्रेजी बोलता है?
kya koi angrezee boltaa hai?
apartment अपार्टमेंट *apartment*
apologize: I apologize
माफी: मैं माफी चाहता हूँ
maafi: main maafi chahtaa hoon
appendicitis अपेंडिसाइटिस
appendicitis
appendix अपेंडिक्स *appendix*
appetite भूख *appetite*
appointment (to make an . . .)
अपॉयन्टमेंट (अपॉयन्टमेंट लेना)
appointment (appointment lena)
approximately लगभग *lugbhug*
April अप्रैल *aprail*
architect आर्किटेक्ट *architect*
are there. . .? क्या . . . हैं?
kya . . . hai?
arm बाँह *baanh*
around लगभग *lugbhug*
arrive, to पहुंचना *pahoonchnaa*
art gallery आर्ट गैलरी *art gallery*
arthritis, to have गठिया होना
gathiyaa hona
artificial sweetener
कृत्रिम मीठा बनाने वाला
kritrim meetha banane waala
artist कलाकार *kalakaar*
ashtray ऐश ट्रे *ash tray*
ask: I asked for
पूछा: मैंने . . . के लिए पूछा
poocha: maine. . .ke liye poocha
aspirin एस्प्रीन *asprin*

asthma, to have दमा होना
  dama hona
at पर *pur*
athletics एथलेटिक्स *athletics*
ATM/cash machine ए टी एम *ATM*
machine मशीन *machine*
attack हमला *humlaa*
attractive आकर्षक *akurshuk*
August अगस्त *agast*
aunt चाची *chachee*
Australia आस्ट्रेलिया *australia*
Australian आस्ट्रेलियन *australian*
authentic: is it authentic?
  वास्तविक: क्या यह वास्तविक है?
  vastavik: kya yeh vastavik hai
authenticity वास्तविकता
  vastaviktaa
automatic
  ~car स्वचालित *swachalit*
  ~camera स्वचालित कैमरा
  swachalit camera
automobile ऑटोमोबाइल
  automobile
autumn शरद *sharad*
avalanche एवालांश *avalanche*
away (from) दूर (से) *door (se)*
awful बेकार *bekaar*

B

baby बच्चा *baccha;*
  ~ food बेबी फूड *baby food;*
  ~ wipes बेबी वाईप्स *baby wipes;*
  ~-sitter बेबी-सिटर *baby sitter*
back पीछे *peeche*
  ~ ache पीठ का दर्द *peeth kaa dard*

backpacking बैक पैकिंग
  back packing
bad बुरा *bura*
bag बैग *bag*
baggage सामान *samaan*
bakery बेकरी *bakery*
balcony बालकनी *balcony*
ball गेंद *gend*
band बैंड *baind*
bandage बैंडेज *bandage*
bank बैंक *bank*
bar बार *bar*
barber नाई *nai*
basement तहखाना *tehkhaana*
basket बास्केट *basket*
basketball बास्केटबॉल
  basketball
bath स्नान *snaan;*
  ~ towel तौलिया *tauliyaa*
bathroom (toilet)
  शौचालय *shauchalaya* (with bath)
  स्नान के साथ *snaan ke saath*
battery बैटरी *battery*
battle site युद्ध स्थल *yudh sthal*
be, to होना *hona*
beach समुद्र-तट *sanudra-tut*
beard दाढ़ी *daadhi*
beautiful खूबसूरत *khubsoorat*
because (of) कारण *kaaran*
bed बिस्तर *bistar*
  ~ and breakfast बिस्तर और
  नाश्ता *bistar aur breakfast*
bedding बिस्तर *bistar*
bedroom शयनकक्ष *shyankaksh*

beer बीयर *beer*
before से पहले *se pehle*
begin, to आरंभ करना
aarambh kurnaa
beige मटमैला *mutmella*
belong: this belongs to me
किसी का होना: यह मेरा है
kisi ka hona:yeh mera hai
belt बेल्ट *belt*
best सबसे अच्छा *sabse acha*
better ज्यादा अच्छा *jyadaa acha*
between बीच में *beech mein*
~ **jobs** नौकरी के बीच में
naukri ke beech mein
bib पीना *peena*
bicycle साइकिल *cycle*;
~ **hire** किराए का साइकिल
kiraaye ka cycle
bidet बिडे *bide*
big बड़ा *bada*
bigger ज्यादा बड़ा *jyadaa bada*
bikini बिकिनी *bikini*
bill बिल *bill*
binoculars दूरबीन *doorbeen*
bird पक्षी *pakshi*
birthday जन्मदिन *janamdin*
biscuits बिस्कुट *biscuit*
bite (insect) काटना *kaatnaa*
bitten: I've been bitten by a dog
काट लिया: मुझे कुत्ते ने काट
लिया ह
kaat liya: mujhe kutte ne kaat liya hai
bitter कड़वा *kadwaa*
bizarre विचित्र *vitchitra*

black काली *kaali*;
~ **and white** श्वेत और श्याम
shwet aur shyam
bladder मूत्राशय *mutrashay*
blanket कंबल *kambal*
bleach ब्लीच *bleach*
bleeding खून बहना *khoon behnaa*
blinds परदा *pardaa*
blister फोड़ा *phodaa*
blocked, to be बाधित, होना
baadhit hona
blood रक्त *rukt*;
~ **group** ब्लड ग्रुप *blood group*;
~ **pressure (high)** रक्तचाप
(उच्च) *ruktchaap (uchh)*
blouse ब्लाउज़ *blouse*
blue नीला *neela*
board, on बोर्ड पर *board pur*
boat नौका *nauka*;
~ **trip** नौका यात्रा *nauka yatra*
boil उबलना *ubulnaa*
boiled उबला *ublaa*
boiler उबालने के लिए बर्त्तन
ubulne ke liye bartan
bone हड्डी *huddi*
book पुस्तक *pustak*;
~ **store** पुस्तक की दुकान
pustak kee dukaan
book, to बुक करना *book kurnaa*
booked up, to be बुक हो चुका
book ho chukaa
booklet of tickets टिकटों की एक
पुस्तिका *tickton kee ek pustak*
boots जूता *jota*

boring विनोदहीन *vinodheen*
born: I was born in
जन्म लेना: मैंने … में जन्म लिया
janam lena: maine…mein janam liya
borrow: may I borrow your?
उधार लेना: क्या मैं आपका उधार ले सकता हूँ?
udhaar lena: kya main aapkaa udhaar le saktaa hoon?
botanical garden
बोटानिकल गार्डन *botanical garden*
bottle बोतल *botal;*
~ **of wine** मदिरा की बोतल
madira kee botal;
~-**opener** बॉटल ऑपनर
bottle opener
bottled बोतलबंद *botulbund*
bowel बोवल *bowel*
bowls कटोरा *katoraa*
box of chocolates चॉकलेट का डब्बा *choclate kaa dubba*
boy लड़का *ladkaa*
boyfriend पुरुष मित्र
purush mitr
bra ब्रा *bra*
bracelet कंगन *kungun*
bread ब्रेड *bread*
bread: loaf of ~ ब्रेड: ब्रेड का लोफ
bread: bread kaa loaf
break, to तोड़ना *todnaa*
break down: the cooker has broken down

खराब होना: कुकर खराब हो गया है
kharaab hona: cooker kharaab ho gaya hai
breakdown खराब होना
kharaab hona;
~ **truck** ब्रेकडाउन ट्रक
breakdown truck; **have a** ~
खराब होना *kharaab hona*
breakfast नाश्ता *nashtaa*
breast स्तन *stun*
breathe, to सांस लेना
saana lena
bridge पुल *pool*
briefs जांघिया *jaanghiyaa*
bring someone, to
किसी को लाना *kissi ko laana*
Britain ब्रिटेन *britain*
British ब्रिटिश *british*
brochure विवरणिका *vivranikaa*
broken, to be टूटना *tootnaa*
bronchitis फेफड़े की सूजन
phephade kee soojan
brooch जड़ाऊ पिन *jadaau pin*
brother भाई *bhai*
brown भूरा *bhoora*
browse, to ब्राउज करना
browse kurnaa
bruise चोट *chot*
bucket बाल्टी *baltee*
Buddha बुद्ध *buddha*
building भवन *bhawan*
built, to be निर्मित होना
nirmit hona

bulletin board बुलेटिन बोर्ड *bulletin board*

bureau de change मुद्रा विनिमय कार्यालय *mudra vinimay karayalaya*

burger बर्गर *burger;* ~ **stand** बर्गर स्टैंड *burger stand*

burn जलना *julnaa*

bus बस *bus;*

~ **route** बस रूट *bus route;*

~ **station** बस स्टेशन *bus station;*

~ **stop** बस स्टाप *bus stop*

business व्यवसाय *vyavasaay;*

~ **class** बिज़नेस श्रेणी *business shrenee;*

~ **trip** कारोबारी यात्रा *karobaari yatra;* **on** ~ व्यवसाय में *vyavasaay mein*

busy व्यस्त *vyast*

butane gas ब्यूटेन गैस *butane gas*

butcher कसाईखाना *kasaaikhaana*

butter मक्खन *mukhan*

button बटन *button*

buy, to खरीदना *khareednaa*

by (near) के पास *ke paas* (time) तक *tuk*

~ **bus** बस द्वारा *bus dwaara;*

~ **car** कार द्वारा *car dwaara;*

~ **ferry** नौका द्वारा *nauka dwaara;*

~ **plane** जहाज द्वारा *jahaaj dwaara;*

~ **train** ट्रेन द्वारा *train dwaara;*

~ **credit card** क्रेडिट कार्ड द्वारा *credit card dwaara*

bye! अलविदा! *alvidaa!*

C

cabin केबिन *cabin*

cable TV केबल टीवी *cable tv*

café कैफे *cafe*

cagoule केगूल *cagoule*

cake केक *cake*

calendar कैलेंडर *calendar*

call, to बात करना *baat karnaa*

~ **collect** कॉल कलैक्ट *call collect;*

~ **for someone** किसी के लिए कॉल *kissi ke liye call*

call the police! पुलिस को बुलाओ! *police ko bulaao*

called: to be called बुलाया गया: बुलाया गया *bulaaya gaya: bulaaya gaya*

camera कैमरा *camera;*

~ **case** कैमरा का खोल *camera kaa khol;*

~ **store** कैमरा की दुकान *camera kee dukan*

camp, to पड़ाव डालना *padaav daalnaa*

campbed कैंप बेड *campbed*

camping कैंपिंग *camping*

campsite कैंप स्थल *camp sthal*

can कैन *can;*

~ **opener** कैन ओपनर *can opener*

Canada कनाडा *canada*

Canadian कनाडावासी *canadawaasi*

cancel, to निरस्त करें *nirast karen*

cancer कैंसर *cancer*

candles मोमबत्ती *mombatti*

candy मिठाई *mithai*

cap टोपी *topi*

car कार *car*

~ **ferry** कार फेरी *car ferry;*

~ **park** कार पार्क *car park;*

~ **rental [hire]** किराए की कार *kiraaye kee car;*

by ~ कार द्वारा *car dwaara*

car (train compartment) कार *car*

carafe सुराही *suraahi*

caravan (trailer) केरावान *caravan*

cards ताश *taash*

careful: be careful!
सावधान: सावधान रहें! *saavdhaan: saavdhaan rahen*

carpet कालीन *kaaleen*

carrier bag ढोने वाला बैग *dhone waala bag*

cart ट्राली *trolley*

carton डब्बा *dubba*

cases खोल *khol*

cash नकद *nakad;*

~ **machine** नकद मशीन *nakad machine*

cash, to नकद पाना *nakad paana*

cashier [cash desk] कैशियर *cashier*

casino कैसिनो *casino*

castle किला *kila*

catch, to (bus) पकड़ना *pakadnaa*

cathedral चर्च *church*

Catholic कैथोलिक *catholic*

cave गुफा *gufaa*

CD सीडी *cd;*

~-**player** सीडी प्लेयर *cd player*

cemetery कब्रिस्तान *kabristaan*

center of town शहर के मध्य *sheher ke madhye*

central heating सेंट्रल हीटिंग *central heating*

ceramics सेरामिक *ceramic*

certificate प्रमाणपत्र *pramaan patra*

chain चेन *chain*

change (coins) बदलें *badlen*

change, to बदलें *badlen*

changing facilities
बदलने की व्यवस्था *badalne kee vyavustha*

chapel गिरजाघर *girijaaghar*

charcoal लकड़ी का कोयला *lakdee kaa koylaa*

charge(s) शुल्क *shulk*

charter flight चार्टर उड़ान *charter udaan*

cheap सस्ता *sustaa*

cheaper और सस्ता *aur sustaa*

check book चेक बुक *check book*

check in, to चेक-इन करना *check-in kurnaa*

check-in desk चेक-इन डेस्क *check-in desk*

check out, to चेक-आउट करना
  check-out karnaa
checkout (supermarket)
  चेक-आउट *check-out*
cheers! मजे करो! *maje karo*
cheese पनीर *paneer*
cheque book चेक बुक *check book*
chess (set) शतरंज (सेट)
  shutranj (set)
chest सीना *seena*
chewing gum च्यूइंग गम
  chewing gum
child बच्चा *buchha;*
  ~ seat बच्चे की सीट
  bucche kee seat
children बच्चे *bucche;*
children's meals बच्चों का भोजन
  bucche kaa bhojan
chocolate चॉकलेट *choclate;*
  ~ bar चॉकलेट बार *choclate bar;*
  ~ ice cream चॉकलेट आइसक्रीम
  choclate ice cream
Christmas क्रिसमस *christmas*
church चर्च *church*
cigarette kiosk सिगरेट की दुकान
  cigarette kee dukaan
cigarettes, packet of
  सिगरेट का पैकेट
  cigarette kaa packet
cigars सिगार *cigar*
cinema सिनेमा *cinema*
claim check क्लेम चेक
  claim check
clean साफ *saaf*

clean, to साफ करना
  saaf kurnaa
cliff चट्टान *chatttan*
clinic चिकित्सालय *chikitsaalya*
cloakroom अमानती सामानघर
  amaantee samaanghar
clock घड़ी *ghadi*
close (near) नजदीक *najdeek*
close, to बंद करना *bund kurnaa*
clothes कपड़े *kapde;*
  ~ pins [pegs] कपड़ों के लिए
  खूँटी *kapdon ke liye khoontee*
clothing store [clothes shop]
  कपड़ों की दुकान
  kapdon kee dukaan
cloudy, to be बदली होना
  badlee hona
clubs (golf) क्लब *club*
coach कोच *coach*
  ~ station कोच स्टेशन
  coach station
coast किनारा *kinaara*
coat कोट *coat;*
  ~ check अमानती सामानघर
  amaantee samaanghar;
  ~ hanger कोट हैंगर
  coat hanger
cockroach तिलचट्टा *tilchatta*
code (area, dialling) कोड (एरिया
  डायलिंग) *code (area dialing)*
coffee कॉफी *coffee*
coin सिक्का *sikka*
cold (adj.) ठंडा *thunda*
cold (flu) सर्दी (फ्लू) *sardee (flu)*

collapse: he's collapsed
बेहोश होना: वह बेहोश हो गया
behosh hona: weh behosh ho gaya

collect, to जमा करना *jama kurna*

color रंग *rang;*
~ **film** रंगीन फिल्म
rangeen film

comb कंघी *kunghee*

come back, to वापस आना
vaapus aana

commission कमीशन *commission*

compact camera कॉम्पैक्ट कैमरा
compact camera

compact disc कॉम्पैक्ट डिस्क
compact disc

company (business) कंपनी
compani (companionship) साथ
saath

compartment (train) कंपार्टमेंट
compartment

composer संगीतकार *sangeetkaar*

computer कंप्यूटर *computer*

concert संगीत-समारोह
sangeet samaroh;
~ **hall** संगीत-समारोह हॉल
sangeet-samaroh hall

concession रिआयत *riyaaut*

concussion: he has ~
रिआयत: उसके पास रिआयत है
riyaaut: uske paas riyaaut hai

conditioner कंडीशनर
conditioner

condoms कंडोम *condom*

conductor कंडक्टर *conductor*

confirm, to निश्चित करें
nishchit karen

congratulations! मुबारक!
mubaarak

connection संपर्क *sampark*

constipation कब्ज *kabz*

consulate कानस्युलेट *consulate*

consult, to परामर्श करना
paramash karnaa

contact lens कॉन्टैक्ट लेंस
contact lens

contact, to संपर्क करना
sampark kurnaa

contagious, to be संक्रामक होना
sunkraamak hona

contain, to रखना *rukhnaa*

contemporary dance
समकालीन नृत्य
samkaaleen nritya

contraceptive गर्भ निरोधक
garbh nirodhuk

cook (n.) रसोइया *rasoiyaa*
(v.) खाना बनाना
khaana banana

cooker कुकर *cooker*

cookies बिस्कुट *biscuit*

cooking खाना बनाना
khanaa banana

coolbox कूल बॉक्स *coolbox*

copper तांबा *tambaa*

copy नकल *nakal*

corkscrew कॉर्क स्क्रू *cork screw*

corner कोना *kona*

correct ठीक *theek*

cosmetics सौंदर्य प्रसाधन
saundarya prasadhan
cot (child's) बिछौना *bichonaa*
cottage कुटिया *kutiyaa*
cotton [cotton wool] कॉटन *cotton*
cough खांसी *khaansee*
cough, to खांसना *khaansnaa*
country (nation) देश *desh*
country music लोक संगीत
lok sangeet
course कोर्स *course*
cousin कजन *cousin*
cover charge कवर शुल्क
cover shulk
cow गाय *gaay*
craft shop शिल्पकला की दुकान
shilpkala kee dukaan
cramps ऐंठन *ainthen*
credit card क्रेडिट कार्ड *credit card;*
~ number नंबर *number*
crib पालना *paalnaa*
crisps कुरकुरे *kurkurre*
crockery क्रॉकरी *crockery*
cross क्रॉस *cross*
cross, to पार करना *paar kurnaa*
crossroad चौराहा *chauraahaa*
crowded भीड़ भाड़ *bheedbhaad*
crown (dental) क्राउन *crown*
cruise (n.) क्रूज़ *cruise*
crutches बैसाखी *baisaakhi*
crystal क्रिस्टल *crystal*
cuisine व्यंजन *vyunjun*
cup प्याला *pyalaa*
cupboard अलमारी *almaari*

currency मुद्रा *mudra;*
~ exchange office
मुद्रा विनिमय कार्यालय
mudraa vinimay karayalaya
curry करी *kari*
curtains परदा *purdaa*
customer service
ग्राहक सेवा *grahak sewa*
customs सीमाशुल्क *seemashulk;*
~ declaration
सीमाशुल्क घोषणापत्र
seemashulk ghoshnaa patra
cut काटना *kaatnaa;*
~ and blowdry कट और ब्लो
ड्राई *cut aur blow dry*
cutlery छुरी-काँटा
choori-kaanta
cycle route साइकिल रास्ता
cycle raasta
cycling साइकिल चालन
cycle challan

D

daily प्रतिदिन *pratidin*
damaged, to be क्षतिग्रस्त होना
shatigrast hona
damp नमी *nami*
dance (n.) नृत्य *nritya*
dancing, to go नृत्य के लिए जाना
nritya ke liye jaana
dangerous खतरनाक
khatarnaak
dark अंधेरा *ndheraa*
daughter बेटी *beti*
dawn उषा काल *usha kaal*

day दिन *din;*

~ **ticket** दिन का टिकट *din kaa ticket;*

~ **trip** दिन की यात्रा *din kee yatra*

dead (battery) मृत (बैटरी) *mrit (battery)*

deaf, to be बहरा होना *behraa hona*

December दिसम्बर *disambar*

deck chair डेक कुर्सी *deck kursee*

declare, to घोषणा करना *ghoshnaa kurnaa*

deduct, to घटाना *ghataana*

deep गहरा *gehraa;*

~ **freeze** डीप फ्रीज *deep freeze*

defrost, to डिफ्रॉस्ट करना *defrost kurnaa*

degrees डिग्री *degree*

delay देरी *deri*

delicatessen तैयार खाने की दुकान *tayaar khaane kee dukaan*

delicious स्वादिष्ट *swadisht*

deliver, to सौंपना *saupnaa*

denim डेनिम *denim*

dental floss डेंटल फ्लॉस *dental floss*

dentist दंत विशेषज्ञ *dunt visheshagay*

dentures दन्तावली *dantawali*

deodorant डिओड्रेंट *deodorant*

depart, to छूटना *chootnaa*

department विभाग *vibhaag*

~ **store** डिपार्टमेंट स्टोर *department store*

departure lounge प्रस्थान विश्राम-कक्ष *prasthan vishraam kaksha*

deposit (security) जमाराशि *jamaraashi*

describe, to विवरण देना *vivrun dena*

destination गंतव्य *gantavaya*

details विस्तृत *vistrit*

detergent डिटरजेंट *detergent*

develop, to (photos) विकसित करना *viksit kurnaa*

diabetes मधुमेह *madhumeh*

diabetic, to be मधुमेह का रोगी होना *madhumeh kaa rogi hona*

diagnosis रोग-निदान *rog-nidaan*

diamond हीरा *heera*

diapers डायपर *diaper*

diarrhea दस्त *dust;*

I have ~ मुझे दस्त है *mujhe dust hai*

dice पांसा *paansaa*

dictionary शब्दकोश *shabdkosh*

diesel डीज़ल *diesel*

diet: I'm on a diet डाइट: मैं डाइट पर हूँ *diet: main diet pur hoon*

difficult मुश्किल *mushkil*

dining: ~ car डाइनिंग: डाइनिंग कार *diating: diating car;*

~ **room** भोजनकक्ष *bhojankaksh*

dinner: to have ~ रात का भोजन: रात का भोजन करना *raat kaa bhojan:raat kaa bhojan;*

~ jacket डाइनिंग जैकेट *dianing jacket*

direct सीधा *seedha*

direction, in the... of दिशा, ... की दिशा में *deesha...deshaa mein*

directions दिशाएं *dishayen*

director (of company) निर्देशक *nirdeshak*

directory (telephone) डायरेक्ट्री *directory*

dirty गंदा *gundaa*

disabled (n.) विकलांग *viklaang*

discotheque डिस्को *disco*

discount छूट *chhoot*

dish व्यंजन *vyunjun;*

~ cloth गुड़िया क्लॉथ *dish cloth*

dishwashing liquid बर्तन धुलाई के लिए द्रव *bartan dhulaai ke liye drawye*

dislocated, to be सरक जाना *sadak jaana*

display cabinet/case प्रदर्शन केबिनेट/केस *pradarshan cabinet/case*

disposable camera डिस्पोजेबल कैमरा *disposable camera*

distilled water डिस्टिल्ड पानी *distilled paani*

disturb: don't disturb परेशान करना: कृपया परेशान ना करें *pareshaan karnaa: kripyaa pareshaan naa karen*

dive, to कूदना *koodnaa*

diversion (detour) मोड़ *mod*

diving equipment गोताखोरी उपकरण *gotakhori upkaran*

divorced, to be तलाकशुदा होना *talaakshudaa hona*

dizzy: I feel dizzy चक्कर आना: मुझे चक्कर आ रहा है *chakkar aana: mujhe chakkar aa raha hai*

do: things to ~ करना: करने योग्य कार्य *karna: karne yogya karyaa;*

what do you do? आप क्या करते हैं? *aap kya karte hain;*

do you accept ...? क्या आप ... स्वीकार करते हैं? *kya aap ... sweekaar karte hain;*

do you have ...? क्या आपके पास ... है? *kya aapke paas ... hai*

doctor चिकित्सक *chikitsak*

doesn't work काम नहीं करता *kaam nahin kurtaa*

doll गुड़िया *gudiyaa*

dollar डॉलर *dollar*

door द्वार *dwaar*

double डबल *double;*

~ bed डबल बेड *double bed*

~ room डबल रूम *double room*

downstairs निचली मंजिल *nichlee manzil*

downtown area डाउनटाउन क्षेत्र
downtown shetre

dozen दर्जन *darzan*

draft [draught] *(beer)* ड्राफ्ट
draft

dress कपड़े *kapde*

drink *(n.)* ड्रिंक *drink*

drinking water पीने का पानी
peene kaa paani

drip, to: the faucet [tap] drips
टपकना: टोंटी टपक रही है
apaknaa: toontee tapak rahi hai

drive, to चलाना *chalana*

driver ड्राइवर *driver*

driver's license ड्राइवर का
लाइसेंस *driver ka license*

drop someone off, to किसी को
छोड़ना *kissi ko chodnaa*

drowning: someone is drowning
डूबना: कोई डूब रहा है *doobnaa:
koi doob raha hai*

drugstore दवाखाना
dawakhaana

drunk नशे में चूर
nashe mein choor

dry cleaner ड्राई क्लिनर
dry cleaner

dry-clean, to ड्राई क्लीन करना
dry clean kurnaa

dubbed, to be
डब करना *dub kurnaa*

during दौरान *dauraan*

dustbins कूड़े का डब्बा
koodhe kaa dubba

duty: to pay duty
ड्यूटी: ड्यूटी देना
duty: duty dena

duvet रजाई *rajaai*

E

e-mail ई-मेल *e-mail;*
~ **address** ई-मेल पता
e-mail pata

ear कान *kaan;*
~ **drops** कान की दवाई
kaan kee dawaai;
~ **ache** कान का दर्द
kaan kaa dard

early जल्दी *jaldee*

earlier पहले *pehlee*

earrings झुमका *jhumkaa*

east पूरब *purub*

Easter ईस्टर *easter*

easy आसान *aasaan*

eat, to भोजन करना
bhojan kurna

economy class इकोनॉमी श्रेणी
economy shreni

eggs अंडे *unde*

elastic *(adj.)* इलास्टिक
elastic

electric: ~ shaver
बिजली: इलेक्टिक शेवर
bijlee: electric shaver

electrical outlets
बिजली का निकास बिंदु
bijlee kaa nikaas bindu

electricity meter
बिजली मीटर *bijlee meter*

electronic: ~ **flash** इलेक्ट्रॉनिक: इलेक्ट्रॉनिक फ्लैश *electronic: electronic flash;*

~ **game** इलेक्ट्रॉनिक खेल *electronic khel;*

~ **items** इलेक्ट्रॉनिक वस्तु *electronic vustu*

elephant हाथी *haathi*

elevator लिफ़्ट *lift*

else: something else अन्य:कुछ और *anya: kuch aur*

email ईमेल *email*

embassy दूतावास *dootavaas*

emerald पन्ना *punna*

emergency आपातकालीन *aapaatkaleen*

emergency exit आपातकालीन निकास *aapaatkaleen nikaas*

empty ख़ाली *khaali*

enamel इनामेल *enamel*

end, to ख़त्म करना *khatam kurnaa*

end: at the end अंत: अंत में *ant: ant mein*

engaged, to be व्यस्त होना *vyast hona*

engine इंजन *engine*

engineering इंजीनियरिंग *engineering*

England इंग्लैंड *england*

English अंग्रेज *angrez*

~-**speaking** अंग्रेजी बोलने वाला *angreji bolne waala*

enjoy, to आनंद लेना *anand lena*

enlarge, to बड़ा करना *bada karna*

enough पर्याप्त *paryapt;*

that's ~ बहुत हो गया *bahut ho gaya*

entertainment guide मनोरंजन गाइड *manoranjan guide*

entrance fee प्रवेश शुल्क *pravesh shulk*

entry visa प्रवेश वीसा *pravesh visa*

envelope लिफाफा *lifafa*

epileptic, to be मिरगी का रोगी होना *mirgee kaa rogee hona*

equipment (sports) उपकरण *upkaran*

error दोष *dosh*

escalator एस्केलेटर *escalator*

essential आवश्यक *aavashyak*

E.U. (European Union) ई.यू. (यूरोपीय संघ) *E.U. (european sangh)*

evening: in the ~ शाम: शाम में *shaam: shaam mein;* ~ **dress** शाम के कपड़े *shaam ke kapde*

events कार्यक्रम *karyakaram*

every: ~ **day** प्रत्येक: प्रतिदिन *pratyek: pratidin;*

~ **hour** प्रति घंटा *prati ghanta*

~ **week** प्रति सप्ताह *prati suptaah*

examination (medical) जाँच *jaanch*

example, for उदाहरणतया *udharantaya*

except सिवाय *sivaay*

excess baggage बहुतायत सामान *bahutayut samaan*

exchange, to अदला-बदली
adlaa-badlee
~ **rate** विनिमय दर *vinimay dur*
excluding meals भोजन के बिना
bhojan ke bina
excursion साहसिक यात्रा
shasik yatra
excuse me (attention) कृपया
ध्यान दें *kripyaa dhyaan dein*
excuse me? (pardon?)
माफ कीजिएगा? *maaf kijiyegaa*
exit निकास *nikaas*
expected, to be आशान्वित रहना
ashanchit rehnaa
expensive मंहगा *mehengaa*
expiration [expiry] date
एक्सपाइरी तिथि *expiry tithi*
exposure (photos) एक्सपोज़र
exposure
express व्यस्त करना *vyakt kurna*
extension एक्सटेंशन *extension*
extra अतिरिक्त *atirikt*
extracted, to be (tooth)
उखड़वाना *ukhaadvana*
eye आंख *aankh*

F

fabric वस्त्र *vastra*
face चेहरा *chehra*
facial फेशियल *facial*
facilities व्यवस्था *vyavustha*
factor (sun cream) फैक्टर *factor*
faint, to feel बेहोशी महसूस
करना *behhoshi mehsoos kurnaa*
fall (season) पतझड़ *putjhad*

family परिवार *parivaar*
famous प्रसिद्ध *praseedh*
fan पंखा *pankha*
far दूर *door;* ~-**sighted**
दूर- दृष्टि *door-drishti;*
how far is it?
यह कितनी दूर पर है?
yeh kitni door pur hai?
fare किराया *kiraya*
farm खेत *khet*
fast फास्ट *fast;*
~ **food** फूड *food;*
~ **food restaurant** फास्ट-शाम
रेस्टोरेंट *fast-food restaurant*
fast, to be (clock)
तेज होना (घड़ी) *tej, hona
(ghaadi)*
fat चर्बी *churbee*
father पिता *pita*
faucet नल *nul*
faulty: this is faulty
खराब: यह खराब है
kharaab: yeh kharaab hai
favorite पसंदीदा *pasandeeda*
fax machine फैक्स मशीन
fax machine
February फरवरी *furvari*
feed, to खाना खिलाना
khaana khilaana
feeding bottle फीडिंग बोतल
feeding bottle
feel ill, to बीमार महसूस करना
bimaar mehsoos kurnaa
female महिला *mahilaa*

ferry फेरी *ferry*

feverish, to feel बुखार महसूस करना *bukhaar mehsoos kurnaa*

few थोड़ा *thodaa*

fiancé(e) मंगेतर *mangetur*

field मैदान *maidaan*

fifth पांचवां *panchwaa*

fight लड़ाई *ladaai*

fill out, to भरें *bharen*

filling (dental) भराई *bharaai*

film फ़िल्म *film*

filter फ़िल्टर *filter*

find, to खोजना *yojnaa*

fine (n.) जुर्माना *jurmaana*

fine (adj.) अच्छा *acha*

finger अंगुली *unglee*

fire: ~ alarm अग्नि: अग्नि अलार्म *agnee: agnee alarm;*
  ~ department [brigade] अग्नि विभाग *agnee vibhaag*
  ~ escape अग्नि से बचाव *agnee se bachav;* **~ extinguisher** अग्नि शामक *agnee shaamak*

there's a fire! वहाँ आग है! *wahan aag hai!*

firewood जरावन *jaravan*

first प्रथम *pratham;*
  ~ class (ticket) प्रथम श्रेणी (टिकट) *pratham shreni (ticket)*

fish restaurant मछली रेस्टोरेंट *uchlee restaurant*

fish store [fishmonger] मछली की दुकान *muchlee kee dukaan*

fit, to फिट होना *fit hona*

fitting room फिटिंग रूम *fitting room*

fix, to दुरुस्त करना *durust kurnaa*

flashlight फ्लैश लाइट *flash light*

flat (puncture) पंचर *puncture*

flavor: what flavors do you have? स्वाद: आपके पास कौन सा स्वाद है? *swaad: aapke paas kaun sa swaad hai?*

flea पिस्सू *pissu*

flight उड़ान *udaan;* **~ number** उड़ान संख्या *udaan sankhya*

flip-flops फ़िलप-फ्लॉप *flip-flop*

floor (level) फ़र्श *fursh*

florist फूल विक्रेता *phooln vikretaa*

flour आटा *aataa*

flower फूल *phool*

flu फ्लू *flu*

flush: the toilet won't flush फ्लश: टॉयलेट में फ्लश नहीं चल रहा। *flush: toilet mein flush nahin chul raha*

fly (insect) मक्खी *mukhi*

foggy, to be कोहरेदार होना *kohredaar hona*

folk art लोक-कला *lok kala*

folk music लोक-संगीत *lok-sangeet*

follow, to अनुकरण करना *anukaran karnaa*

food भोजन *bhojan;* **~ poisoning** विषैले भोजनपान की बीमारी *vishella bhojanpaan ki bimaari*

foot पैर *pair*; ~ **path** पगडंडी *pugdundee*
football फुटबॉल *football*
for के लिए *ke liye*
~ **a day** एक दिन के लिए *ek din ke liye*;
~ **a week** एक सप्ताह के लिए *ek saptaah ke liye*
forecast पूर्वानुमान *purvanamaan*
foreign currency विदेशी मुद्रा *videshi mudra*
forest जंगल *jungle*
forget, to भुल जाना *bhool jaana*
fork कांटा *kaanta*
form फॉर्म *form*
formal dress नियमानुसार कपड़े *niymnusaar kapde*
fortnight पाक्षिक *paakshik*
fortunately सौभाग्यवश *saubhagyavash*
fountain फव्वारा *phavaaraa*
four-door car चार दरवाजे वाली कार *chaar durwaaje waali car*
four-wheel drive फोर व्हील ड्राईव *four wheel drive*
fourth चतुर्थ *chaturth*
foyer फॉएर *foyer*
fracture फ्रेक्चर *fracture*
frame (glasses) फ्रेम *frame*
free फ्री *free*
freezer फ्रीज़र *freezer*
frequent: how frequent? आवृति: कितनी बार? *aavriti: kitni baar?*

frequently अक्सर *aksar*
fresh ताजा *fresh*
Friday शुक्रवार *shukravaar*
fried तले हुआ *tale hua*
friend मित्र *mitr*
friendly मित्रतापूर्वक *mitrataapurvak*
fries फ्राई *fries*
frightened, to be डर जाना *dur jaana*
from (come from) से *se*
front सामने *saamne*; ~ **door** सामने का द्वार *saamne ka dwaar*
frosty, to be पालेदार होना *paaledaar hona*
frying pan तलने के लिए बर्तन *talne ke liye bartan*
fuel इंधन *indhun*
full पूर्ण *purun*;
~ **board** (American Plan [A.P.]) पूर्ण भोजन *purun bhojan*
~ **insurance** पूर्ण बीमा *purun beema*
fun, to have मस्ती करना *masti karma*
furniture फर्नीचर *furniture*
further और *aur*
fuse फ्यूज़ *fuse*;
~ **box** फ्यूज़ बॉक्स *fuse box*

G

gallon गैलन *gallon*
game (soccer, etc.) खेल *khel*
game (toy) खेल *khel*
garage गैराज *garage*

garbage bags कूड़े की थैली
koode kee theli
garden बगीचा *bageecha*
gas: I smell gas!
गैस: मुझे गैस की गंध आ रही है!
gas: mujhe gas ki gundh aa rahi hai;
~ bottle गैस की बोतल
gas ki botal
gas station गैस स्टेशन *gas station*
gasoline गैसोलीन *gasoline*
gate *(airport)* द्वार *dwaar*
gauze बैंडेज *bandage*
gay club समलैंगिक क्लब
sumlaingik club
genuine असली *aslee*
get, to पाना *paana*
~ off चले जाओ *chalo jao;*
~ to *(reach)* पहुंचो *pahooncho;*
how do I get to? मैं … तक
कैसे पहुँचुंगा? *main…tuk kaise
pahoonchugaa*
gift उपहार *uphaar;*
~ store उपहार की दुकान
uphaar ki dukaan
girl लड़की *ladki*
girlfriend महिला मित्र *mahila mitr*
give, to देना *dena*
give way *(yield)* रास्ता देना
rastaa dena
gland ग्रन्थि *granthi*
glass गिलास *gilaas*
glasses *(optical)* चश्मा *chushma*
glossy finish चमकीली फिनिश
chumkeela finish

glove दस्ताना *dustaana*
go: to ~ to जाओ: पर जाओ
jao: pur jao
let's ~! चलो चलें! *chalo chalen*
~ away! दूर चले जाओ!
door chale jao
goggles धूप का चश्मा
dhoop ka chushmaa
gold सोना *sona;*
~-plate सोने का प्लेट
sone ka plate
golf गोल्फ *golf;*
~ course गोल्फ कोर्स *golf course*
good अच्छा *acha*
~ morning सुप्रभात *suprabhaat;*
~ afternoon नमस्ते *namaste;*
~ evening नमस्ते *namaste;*
~ night शुभरात्रि *shubhratri;*
~ value अच्छा मूल्य *acha mulya*
~ bye नमस्ते *namaste*
gram *(weight)* ग्राम *gram*
grandparents *(paternal)* दादा-दादी
/ *(maternal)* नाना-नानी *dada-
dadi/nana-nani*
grapes अंगूर *angoor*
grass घास *ghaas*
gray भूरा *bhoora*
graze *(cut)* खरोंच *kharonch*
great *(excellent)* बहुत बढ़िया
bahut badhiyaa
great *(good idea)* महान *mahaan*
green हरा *hara*
greengrocer सब्जियों की दुकान
subjeeyon kee dukaan

grilled ग्रिल्ड *grilled*

grocer किराने की दुकान
kiraane ki dukaan

ground *(earth)* जमीन *zameen*

~ cloth [~sheet] पोछा *poucha*

group समूह *samooh*

guarantee गारंटी *guarantee*

guide *(tour)* गाइड *guide*

guidebook स्थान सूचक पुस्तक
sthan soochak pustak

guided tour मार्ग-दर्शित भ्रमण
marg-darshit brahman

guided walk/hike
मार्ग-दर्शित पैदल चालान/सैर
marg-darshit paidal/chaalan

guitar गिटार *guitar*

gum गोंद *gond*

guy rope रस्सी *russi*

gynecologist स्त्री रोग विशेषज्ञ
stree rog visheshyagya

H

hair बाल *baal;* **~ mousse/gel**
हेयर मूस/जेल *hair mousse/gel;*
~ spray हेयर स्प्रे *hair spray;*
~cut बाल कटाई *baal kataai*

hairdresser हेयर डेसर *hair dresser*

hammer हथौड़ा *hathodaa*

hand हाथ *haath;*
~ luggage हैंडबैग *handbag;*
~ washable हाथ से धोने योग्य
haath se dhone yogya

handbag हैंडबैग *handbag*

handicapped, to be
पंगु होना *pungu hona*

handicrafts हस्तशिल्प *hasthshilp*

handkerchief रुमाल *rumaal*

hanger हैंगर *hanger*

hangover हैंगओवर *hangover*

**happy: I'm not happy with the
service** खुश: मैं सेवा से खुश नहीं
हूँ *khush: main sewa se khush
nahin hoon*

harbor बंदरगाह *bandargaah*

hat हैट *hat*

have है *hai*

can I have? क्या मुझे मिल सकता
है? *kya mujhe mil saktaa hai*
~ to क्या मुझे करना जरूरी है
kya mujhe kurna zaroori hai;
~ an appointment क्या मुझे
अपॉयन्टमेंट मिल सकता है *kya
mujhe appointment mil sakti hai*

hayfever बुखार *bukhaar*

head मुख्य *mukhya;*
~ waiter मुख्य वेटर *mukhya
waiter*
~ ache सिर दर्द *sir dard*

heading, to be बढ़ना *badna*

health food store हेल्थ फूड स्टोर
health food store

hear, to सुनना *sunna*

hearing aid हिअरिंग ऐड
hearing aid

heart हृदय *hridya;*
~ attack दिल का दौरा *dil kaa
daura;*
~ condition हृदय रोग *hridya rog*

hearts *(cards)* पान *paan*

heater हीटर *heater*

heating गर्म करना *garm karnaa*

heavy भारी *bhaari*

height ऊंचाई *unchaai*

hello नमस्ते *namaste*

help: can you help me? सहायता: क्या आप मेरी सहायता कर सकते हैं? *sahaytaa: kya aap meri sahaytaa kur sakte hain*

hemorrhoids बवासीर *bawasir*

her उसकी *uski*

here यहाँ *yahan*

hernia हर्निया *hernia*

hers उसका *uskaa*; **it's hers** यह उसका है *yeh uska hai*

hi! नमस्ते! *namaste*

high उच्च *ucch*

highlight, to (hair) हाईलाइट करना *highlight kurna*

highway हाइवे *highway*

hike (n.) सैर *sair*

hiking सैर *sair*; ~ **boots** सैर करने वाला जूता *sair karne waala jota*

hill पहाड़ी *pahadi*

hire, to किराए ij ysuk **kiraye** pur lena

his उसका *uska*; **it's his** यह उसका है *yeh uska hai*

hitchhiking लिफ्ट मांगना *lift mangnaa*

HIV-positive एच आइ वी-पॉज़िटिव *HIV-positive*

hobby शौक *shauk*

hold on, to पकड़े रहना *pakde rehnaa*

hole छिद्र *chidr*

holiday: on ~ छुट्टी: छुट्टी पर *chutti: chutti pur*; ~ **resort** हॉलिडे रिसॉर्ट *holiday resort*

home: we're going home घर: हमलोग घर जा रहे हैं *ghar: hum log jaa rahen hain*

homosexual समलैंगिक *sumlaingik*

honeymoon: we're on honeymoon हनीमून: हम लोग हनीमून पर हैं *honeymoon: hum log honeymoon pur hain*

hopefully आशापूर्वक *aashapurvak*

horse घोड़ा *ghodaa*; ~ **racing** घुड़दौड़ *ghuddaud*

hospital अस्पताल *aspataal*

hot गर्म *garm*; ~ **dog** हॉट डॉग *hot dog*; ~ **spring** गर्म सोता *garm sota*; ~ **water** गर्म पानी *garm paani*

hotel होटल *hotel*

hour घंटा *ghuntaa*; **in an ~** एक घंटे में *ek ghunte mein*

house घर *ghar*

housewife गृहिणी *grahini*

hovercraft हॉवर क्राफ्ट *hover craft*

how? कैसे? *kaise*

how are you? आप कैसे हैं?
aap kaise hain
how far…? कहाँ तक …?
kahan tuk…
how long…? कब तक …?
kub tuk…
how many…? कितनी बार …?
kitnee baar…
how much? (money) कितने? *kitne*
how much? (quantity) कितनी?
kitnee
how often? कितनी बार?
kitnee baar
how old? कितना पुराना?
kitnaa puranna
hundred सौ *sau;*
~thousand लाख *lakh*
hungry: I'm hungry
भूखा होना: मैं भूखा हूँ
bhook hona: main bhookha hoon
hurry: I'm in a hurry
जल्दी: मैं जल्दी में हूँ
jaldee: main jaldee mein hoon
hurt, to चोट पंहुचाना *chot
pahoonchnaa;* **my** मेरा *mera;*
hurts: दर्द करता है *dard kurta hai;*
to be hurt चोट *gksuk chot hona*
husband पति *pati*

I

I'd like मैं पसंद करुंगा
main pasand karoonga
I'll have मैं लूंगा *main loonga*
ice बर्फ *burf*

ice cream आइसक्रीम *ice cream;*
~ parlor आइसक्रीम पार्लर
ice cream parlour
icy, to be बर्फीला होना
burfeela hona
identification पहचान *pehchaan*
ill: I'm ill बीमार: मैं बीमार हूँ
bimaar: main bimaar hoon
illegal: is it illegal?
गैरकानूनी: यह गैरकानूनी है?
gair kanooni: yeh gair kanooni hai
imitation नकल *nakal*
immediately तुरंत *turunt*
in में *mein*
included: is included?
शामिल: क्या यह शामिल है?
shaamil: kya yeh shaamil hai
India भारत *bharat*
indicate, to दर्शाना *durshaana*
indigestion बदहजमी
badhhuzmee
indoor pool इंडोर पूल *indoor pool*
inexpensive सस्ता *sustaa*
infected, to be संक्रमित होना
sankraamit hona
infection संक्रमण *sankraman*
inflammation of की जलन *kee
zalan*
informal अनौपचारिक
anopchaareek
information सूचना *soochnaa;*
~ desk सूचना डेस्क *soochnaa
desk;* **~ office** सूचना कार्यालय
soochnaa karalaya

Information (telephone service)
सूचना *soochnaa*
injection सुई *sui*
injured, to be घायल होना
ghayal hona
innocent नादान *naadaan*
insect कीड़ा *keera;*
    ~ bite कीड़े का काटना
    keere kaa kaatnaa;
    ~ repellent कीड़ा भगाने वाला
    keera bhagane waala
inside अंदर *andar*
insist: I insist दृढ़ होना: मैं दृढ़ हूँ
    dridh hona: main dridh hoon
insomnia नींद ना आने की बीमारी
    neend naa aane kee bimaaree
instant coffee इंस्टेंट कॉफी
    instant coffee
instead of सिवाय *siwaay*
instructions निर्देश *nirdesh*
instructor अध्यापक *adhyapak*
insulin इंसुलिन *insulin*
insurance बीमा *beema;*
    ~ card बीमा कार्ड *bema card;*
    ~ claim बीमा दावा *bema dawa*
interest (hobby) रुचि *ruchi*
interesting रुचिकर *rucheekur*
International Student Card
    अंतर्राष्ट्रीय स्टुडेंट कार्ड
    anturrashtriya student card
Internet इंटरनेट *internet*
interpreter अनुवादक
    anuvaaduk
intersection चौराहे *chaurahe*

introduce oneself, to
    अपना परिचय दें *apnaa parichay
    dein*
invitation आमंत्रण *aamantran*
invite, to आमंत्रित करें
    aamantrit karen
involved, to be शामिल होना
    shaamil hona
iodine आयोडिन *iodine*
Ireland आयरलेंड *Ireland*
Irish आयरिश *irish*
is: is it? है: है कि नहीं?
    hai: hai ki nahin
is there? क्या? *kya*
is this? क्या यह? *kya yeh*
it is यह है *yeh hai*
Italian (cuisine) इतालवी *itaalvee*
itch: it itches
    खुजली: यह खुजलाता है
    khujlee: yeh khujultaa hai
itemized bill आइटमाइज्ड बिल
    itemized bill

J

jacket जैकेट *jacket*
jam जैम *jam*
jammed, to be जाम होना
    jaam hoona
January जनवरी *janvari*
Japan जापान *japan*
Japanese जापानी *japanee*
jar डब्बा *dubba*
jaw जबड़ा *jubdaa*
jazz जैज *jazz*
jeans जींस *jeans*

jellyfish जेलीफिश *jellyfish*

jet lag: I'm jet lagged
जेट लैग: मुझे जेट लैग है
jet lag: mujhe jet lag hai

jet-ski जेट स्की *jet ski*

jeweler जौहरी *johree*

joke मजाक *majaak*

journalist पत्रकार *patrakaar*

journey यात्रा *yatraa*

jug (of water) जग *jug*

July जुलाई *july*

jump leads जंप लीड्स *jump leads*

jumper जंपर *jumper*

junction (intersection) जंक्शन
junction

June जून *june*

K

keep: keep the change!
रखें: खुल्ले रख लीजिए!
rakhen: khulle rukh lijiye

kerosene किरासिन *kerosene;*
~ stove किरासिन का चूल्हा
kerosene kaa chulhaa

ketchup केचप *ketchup*

kettle केतली *ketlee*

key चाबी *chaabee;* **~ ring** चाबी
का गुच्छा *chaabee kaa guchha*

kiddie pool खेलने के लिए छोटा
तालाब *khelne ke liye chota talaab*

kidney गुर्दा *gurdaa*

kilogram किलोग्राम *kilogram*

kilometer किलोमीटर *kilometer*

kind (pleasant) सुहाना *suhana*

kind: what kind of
प्रकार: किस प्रकार का
prakaar: kis prakaar kaa

kiss, to चुंबन लेना *chumbun lena*

kitchen रसोईघर *rasoi ghar*

knapsack झोला *jhola*

knee घुटना *ghutnaa*

knickers निकर्स *knickers*

knife चाकू *chaaku*

know: I don't know
जानना: मैं नहीं जानता
jaannaa: main nahin jaantaa

Korea कोरिया *korea*

Korean कोरियाई *koreaai*

kosher कोशर *kosher*

L

label लेबल *label*

lace फीता *pheeta*

ladder सीढ़ी *seedhe*

lake झील *jheel*

lamp लैंप *lamp*

land, to उतरना *uturnaa*

language course भाषा कोर्स
bhasha course

large बड़ा *bada*

larger ज्यादा बड़ा *jyadaa bada*

last अंतिम *anteem*

last, to समाप्त होना *samapt hona*

late देर (देरी होना) *der (deri hona)*

later बाद में *baad mein*

laugh, to हंसना *hansnaa*

laundromat लौंड्रोमैट
Laundromat

laundry: ~ facilities
कपड़ा धुलाई: कपड़ा धुलाई
व्यवस्था
*kapdaa dhulaai: kapdaa dhulaai
vyavustha;*
~ **service** कपड़ा धुलाई सेवा
kapdaa dhulaai sewa
lavatory प्रसाधन कक्ष *prasadhun
kaksh*
lawyer वकील *vakeel*
laxative शिथिल करने वाला
sheetheel karne wala
lead, to (road) मार्ग दिखलाना
maarg dikhlana
leader नेता *neta*
leak, to टपकना *tapaknaa*
learn, to सीखना *seekhnaa*
leather चमड़ा *chamdaa*
leave, to (deposit)
जमाराशि *jamaraashi*
(person) छोड़ना *chhomaa*
(aircraft) से जाना *se jaanaa*
leave me alone!
मुझे अकेला छोड़ दो!
mujhe akelaa chhod do
left: on the ~ बाएं: बाएं में
bayan: bayan mein
left-luggage office खोया सामान
कार्यालय *khoya saaman karyalay*
leg पैर *pair*
legal: is it legal?
कानूनी: क्या यह कानूनी है?
kanoonee: kya yeh kanoonee hai

leggings लेगिंग्स *leggings*
lemon नींबू *neembu*
lemonade लेमोनेड *lemonade*
lend: could you lend me? उध
ार देना: क्या आप मुझे उधार दे
सकते हैं?
*udhaar dena: kya aap mujhe udhaar
de sakte hain*
length (of) लंबाई (का)
lumbaai (kaa)
lens लेंस *lens*
~ **cap** लेंस कैप *lens cap*
lesbian club लेसबियन क्लब
lesbian club
less कम *kum*
lesson पाठ *path*
let: let me know! करने देना: मुझे
बताओ! *karne dena: mujhe batao*
letter पत्र *patra;*
~ **box** पत्र पेटी *patra peti*
level (even ground) स्तर *stur*
library पुस्तकालय *pustakalaya*
lie down, to लेट जाना *let jaana*
lifeboat जीवन-रक्षक नौका
jeevan–rakshak nauka
lifeguard जीवन-रक्षक
jeevan–rakshak
lifejacket जीवन-रक्षक जैकेट
jeevan–rakshak jacket
life preserver [belt] बेल्ट *belt*
lift (elevator) लिफ्ट *lift*
lift (hitchhiking) लिफ्ट लेना
lift lena

light (electric) लाइट *light;* **~ bulb**
लाइट बल्ब *light bulb*
~ color हल्का *hulkaa*
~ weight हल्का *hulkaa;*
lighter (color) ज्यादा हल्का
jyadaa hulka; (cigarette) लाइटर
(सिगरेट)
like: ~ this समान: इसके समान
samaan: iske samaan
like, to पसंद करना *pasand kurnaa*
I like it मैं पसंद करता हूँ
main pasand karta hoon
I don't like it मैं पसंद नहीं करता हूँ
main pasand nahin kartaa hoon
I'd like मैं पसंद करूंगा
main pasand karoongaa
limousine लिमोज़िन *limousine*
line (subway [metro]) लाईन *line*
linen लिनेन *linen*
lip होंठ *honth;*
~ stick लिपस्टिक *lipstick*
liqueur मीठी सुगन्धित शराब
meethi sugandhit sharaab
liquor store शराब की दुकान
sharaab kee dukaan
liter लीटर *liter*
little छोटा *chhota*
live, to जीना *jeena;*
~ together साथ जीना
saath jeena
liver कलेजा *kaleja*
living room लिविंग रूम
living room
lobby लॉबी *lobby*

local स्थानीय *sthaniye*
~ anaesthetic
स्थानीय असंवेदनता की दवा
sthaniye asunvedantaa kee dawaa
lock, to ~ oneself out
बंद, अपने को बाहर बंद कर लेना
bund, apne ko baahar bund kur lena
log on, to लॉग आन करना
log aan kurnaa
long लंबा *lambaa;*
~-distance लंबी दूरी
lambee doori;
~-sighted दूर दृष्टि दोष
door drishti dosh;
how long कितना लंबा
kitnaa lumba
look: I'm just looking
देखो: मैं सिर्फ देख रहा हूँ
dekho: main sirf dekh raha hoon;
look like समान दिखना
samaan dikhna;
to be looking for
देखना लिए *dekhna liye*
loose ढीला *dheela*
lorry लॉरी *lorry*
lose, to ढीला करना *dheela karma*
I've lost मैं खो चुका हूं
main kho chukka hoon
lost-and-found office
[lost property office]
खोया-और-पाया कार्यालय
khoya aur paayaa karyalaya
lots of fun बहुत सारा मजा
bahut saara maza

louder ज्यादा तेज आवाज़
jyadaa tez aawaaz
love: I love you प्यार: मैं तुम्हें प्यार
करता हूं *pyaar: main tumhe pyaar
kurta hoon*
lovely प्यारा *pyaara*
low निम्न *nimn;*
~ **bridge** नीचा पुल *neecha pul;*
~-**fat** कम चर्बी *kum churbee*
luck: good luck भाग्य: सौभाग्य
bhagaya: saubhagaya
luggage सामान *samaan;*
~ **cart [trolley]**
सामान की ट्राली *samaan ki trolley*
~ **locker** अमानती सामानघर
amaantee samaanghar
lump सूजन *soojun*
lunch दोपहर का भोजन
dopaher kaa bhojan
lung फेफड़ा *phephdaa*

M

machine washable
मशीन से धोने योग्य
machine se dhone yogya
madam मैडम *madam*
magazine पत्रिका *patreekaa*
magnificent शानदार
shaandaar
maid नौकरानी *naukraani*
mail (n.) चिट्ठी *chitthi;*
by~ चिट्ठी द्वारा *chitthi dwarra;*
~ **box** पत्र पेटी *patra peti;*
(v.) चिट्ठी भेजना
chitthi bhejnaa

main मुख्य *mukhya;*
~ **street** मुख्य सड़क *mukhya
sadak*
make an appointment, to
अपॉयंटमेंट लेना *appointment lena*
make-up श्रृंगार *shringaar*
male पुरुष *purush*
mallet लकड़ी का हथौड़ा
lakdee kaa hathodaa
man पुरुष *purush*
manager प्रबंधक *prabundhuk*
manicure मेनीक्योर *manicure*
manual (car) मेन्यूअल *manual*
map नक्शा *naksha*
March मार्च *march*
margarine कृत्रिम मक्खन
kritrim makhan
market बाजार *bazaar*
married, to be शादीशुदा होना
shaadi shudaa hona
mascara मैसकारा *mascara*
mask (diving) नकाब *nakaab*
mass सभा *sabha*
massage मालिश *maalish*
match (soccer, etc.) मैच *match*
matches मैचों *matchon*
matineé अपरान्ह का शो
apraahan
matter: it doesn't matter
विषय: यह मायने नहीं रखता
vishay: yeh maayne nahin rakhta
what's the matter? क्या बात है?
kya baat hai
mattress गद्दा *guddha*

May मई *mai*

may I? क्या मैं? *kya main*

maybe शायद *shaayad*

me मुझे *mujhe*

mean, to मतलब *mutlub*

measles खसरा *khusraa*

measure, to मापना *maapnaa*

measurement माप *map*

meat मांस *maans*

medical certificate मेडीकल प्रमाण पत्र *medical pramanpatra*

medication इलाज *ilaaj*

medium मध्यम *madhyam*

meet, to मिलना *milnaa*

pleased to meet you आप से मिल कर खुशी हुई *aap se mil kur khushi hui*

meeting place [point] मिलने की जगह *milne kee jagah*

member सदस्य *sadasya*

men (toilets) पुरुष *purush*

mention: don't mention it चर्चा: कृपया चर्चा ना करें *churcha: kripyaa churchaa naa Karen*

menu मेनू *menu*

message संदेश *sandesh*

metal धातु *dhaatu*

meter (in taxi) मीटर *meter*

metro मेट्रो *metro;* \
~ station मेट्रो स्टेशन *metro station*

microwave माइक्रोवेव *microwave*

midday मध्यान्ह *madhyah*

midnight मध्यरात्रि *madhyaratree*

migraine माइग्रेन *migraine*

mileage माइलेज *mileage*

milk दूध *dhoodh;*
with ~ दूध के साथ *dhoodh ke saath*

million दस लाख *dus lakh*

mind: do you mind if ...? बुरा मानना: आपको बुरा तो नहीं लगेगा अगर ... ? *bura manna: aapko bura to nahin lagega agur...*

mine मेरा *mera;*
it's mine! यह मेरा है! *yeh mera hai*

mineral water मिनरल वाटर *mineral water*

mini-bar मिनी-बार *mini-bar*

minimart मिनी-मार्ट *mini-mart*

minute मिनट *minute*

mirror आईना *ainaa*

missing, to be खो जाना *kho jaana*

mistake गलती *galtee*

mobile home चलनशील घर *chalansheel ghar*

modern आधुनिक *aadhunik*

moisturizer मॉश्चराइजर *moisturizer*

monastery मठ *muth*

Monday सोमवार *somvaar*

money धन *dhun;*
~ order मनी ऑर्डर *money order*

month महीना *mahinaa;*

monthly मासिक *maasik*

moped मोपेड *moped*

more और *aur;*
  I'd like some more …
  मुझे कुछ और … चाहिए
  mujhe kuch aur chahiye…

morning, in the सुबह में
  subah mein

mosque मस्जिद *masjid*

mosquito bite मच्छर का काटना
  machchhar ka katna

mosquito मच्छर *machchhar*

mosquito net मच्छरदानी
  machchhardani

mother माँ *maa*

motion sickness गति संबंध
  री बीमारी *gati sambhundhee*
  bimaaree

motorbike मोटरबाइक
  motorbike

motorboat मोटरबोट *motorboat*

motorway मोटरवे *motorway*

mountain पर्वत *parvat;*
  ~ bike पर्वतीय साइकिल
  parvatiye cycle;
  ~ pass पर्वतीय रास्ता
  parvartiye raasta;
  ~ range पर्वतीय श्रृंखला
  parvartiye shrinkhlaa

moustache मूँछ *mooch*

mouth मुँह *moonh;*
  ~ ulcer मुँह का अल्सर
  moonh kaa ulcer

move, to हिलना *hilnaa;*
  don't move him! उसे मत
  हिलाओ! *use mut hilao*

movie सिनेमा *cinema;*
  ~ theater सिनेमा थियेटर
  cinema theater

Mr. श्रीमान् *shrimaan*

Mrs. श्रीमती *shrimatee*

much ज़्यादा *jyaada*

mugged, to be हमला होना
  humlaa hona

mugging हमला *humlaa*

mugs मग *mug*

multiple journey बहु यात्रा
  bahu yaatra

multiplex cinema
  मल्टीप्लेक्स सिनेमा
  multiplex cinema

mumps मंप्स *mumps*

muscle माँसपेशी *maanspeshi*

museum संग्रहालय *sanghralaya*

music संगीत *sangeet*

musician संगीतकार *sangeetkaar*

must: I must होना: मुझे … चाहिए
  hona: mujhe …chahiye

mustard सरसों *sarson*

my मेरा *mera*

myself: I'll do it myself
  स्वयं: मैं यह स्वयं करूंगा
  wain: main yeh swain karoongaa

N

name नाम *naam;*
  my name is मेरा नाम है
  mera naam hai;
  what's your name?
  आपका नाम क्या है?
  aapkaa naam kya hai;

what's your surname?
आपका उपनाम क्या है?
aapkaa upnaam kya hai

napkin नैपकीन *napkin*

nappies नैपिज *nappies*

narrow संकरा *sunkraa*

national राष्ट्रीय *rashtriya*

nationality राष्ट्रीय
rashtriyeetaa

nature reserve
प्राकृतिक संपदा
prakritik sampadaa

nausea जी मचलाहट
jee muchlaahut

near निकट *nikut*

  ~-sighted निकट दृष्टि *nikut drishtee*

nearest निकटतम *nikuttum*

nearby आसपास *aaspaas*

necessary आवश्यक *aavshayak*

neck गर्दन *gurdan*

necklace माला *maala*

nephew भतीजा/भांजा
bhatijaa/bhaanjaa

nerve नस *nus*

nervous system नाड़ी-मंडल
naadi–mundal

never कभी नहीं *kabhi nahin;*
  ~ mind बुरा ना मानें
bura naa maane

new नया *naya*

New Year नया साल *naya saal*

New Zealand न्यूजीलैंड
new zealand

New Zealander न्यूजीलैंड वासी
new zealand vaasi

newspaper समाचार पत्र
samachar patra

newsstand [newsagent]
समाचारपत्र की दुकान
samachaar patra kee dukaan

next अगला *aglaa*

next to... के बाद ... *ke baad...*

next stop! अगला स्टॉप
aglaa stop

nice अच्छा *acha*

niece भतीजी/भांजी
bhatijee/bhaanjee

night: at ~ रात: रात में *raat: raat mein;* **~-club** नाइट क्लब *night club*

no नहीं *nahin*

no one कोई नहीं *koi nahin*

no way! हरगिज़ नहीं! *hargeej nahin*

noisy कोलाहलपूर्ण *kolahulpurn*

non-alcoholic अलकोहल रहित
alcohol rahit

non-smoking गैर- धूम्रपान
gair dhrumpaan

none एक भी नहीं *ek bhi nahin*

nonsense! बकवास! *bukwaas*

noon मध्यान्ह *mudhyaan*

normal सामान्य *saamaanyaa*

north उत्तर *uttar*

nose नाक *naak*

not: not bad नहीं: बुरा नहीं
nahin: bura nahin

not good अच्छा नहीं *acha nahin*

not yet अभी तक नहीं *abhi tuk nahin*

note संकेत *sanket*

nothing else और कुछ नहीं *aur kuch nahin*

notify, to सूचना देना *soochnaa dena*

November नवंबर *navambar*

now अब *ab*

numbers संख्या *sankhyaa*

number plate नंबर प्लेट *number plate*

nurse देखभाल *dekhbaal*

nylon नाइलोन *nylon*

O

o'clock: it's ... o'clock बजे: अभी ... बजा है *baje: abhi ... baja hai*

occasionally कभी-कभी *kabhi-kabhi*

occupied व्यस्त *vyast*

October अक्तूबर *uctoober*

odds IEeHkkouk *sambhaavnaa*

of course बिल्कुल *bilkul*

off licence गैर लाइसेंसी *gair licensee*

off-peak सामान्य काल *samanya kaal*

office कार्यालय *karayalaya*

often अक्सर *aksar*

oil तेल *tel*

okay ठीक *theek*

old पुराना *puraanaa*

~ town पुराना शहर *puraana sheher;*

~-fashioned पुराने फैशन का *puraane fashion kaa*

olive oil जैतून का तेल *jaitoon kaa tel*

omelet ऑमलेट *omelet*

on में *mein;*

~ foot पैदल *paidal;*

~ my own अपने बलबूते *apne balbutte;*

~ the hour समय पर *samy pur;*

~ the left बाएं की ओर *bayan ki aur;* **~ the other side** दूसरी दिशा में *doosree dishaa mein;*

~ the right दाहिने की ओर *dahine kee aur;*

~ the spot स्थल पर *sthal pur*

on/off switch चालू/बंद चरम *chaalu/bund switch*

once एकबार *ek baar*

one: ~-way एक: एकतरफा *ek: ektarfaa;*

~-way street एकतरफा सड़क *ektarfaa sadak;*

~-way ticket एकतरफा टिकट *ektarfaa ticket;*

~ like that उस तरह का *us tarah kaa*

open खुला *khulla*

open, to खोलना *kholnaa*

opening hours खुले रहने का समय *khule rehne kaa samay*

opera संगीत नाटक *sangeet natak;*

~ house संगीत नाट्यशाला
sangeet natayashaala
operation शल्य चिकित्सा
shulya chikitsaa
opposite विरुद्ध *veerudh*
optician ऑप्टिशियन *optician*
or या *yaa*
orange संतरा *santraa*
orchestra आर्केस्ट्रा *orchestra*
order, to ऑर्डर करना *order karnaa*
organized hike/walk संगठित
सैर/पैदल चालन *sangatith sair/*
paidal chulnaa
our(s) हमारा *hamaraa*
outdoor आउटडोर *outdoor*
outrageous निर्लज्ज *nirluj*
outside बाहर *baahar*
oval अंडाकार *undakaar*
oven चूल्हा *chulhaa*
over there वहाँ पर *wahan pur*
overcharge: I've been
overcharged अधिक मूल्य लेना:
मुझ से अधिक मूल्य ले लिया
गया है *adhik mulya lena: mujh se*
adhik mulya le liya gaya hai
overdone अधिक पका *adhik paka*
overheat अधिक गर्म
adhik garam
overnight रात भर में *raat bahr*
mein
owe, to ऋणी होना *rinee hona;*
how much do I owe?
मुझे कितना देना है?
mujhe kitna dena hai

own: on my own अपना: अपने
बलबूते *apna: apne bulbute*
owner स्वामी *swami*

P

p.m. अपराह्न *apraahan*
pacifier शांत‍श करने वाला
shaant karne waala
pack, to भरना *bhurnaa*
package पुलिन्दा *pulindaa*
packed lunch बंद दोपहर का
भोजन *bund dopaher kaa bhojan*
packet of cigarettes सिगरेट का
डब्बा *cigarette ka dubba*
padlock ताला *taala*
pail बाल्टी *baaltee*
pain: to be in दर्द: दर्द में होना
dard: dard mein hona;
~ killers दर्दनाशक
dardnaashak
paint, to चित्रकारी करना
chitrakaari karnaa
painter चित्रकार *chitrakaar*
painting चित्रकला *chitrkalaa*
pair of, a एक जोड़ी *ek jodi*
palace महल *mahal*
palpitations धड़कन *dhadkan*
panorama चित्रावली *chitravali*
pants पैंट *pant*
pantyhose पैंटीहोज़ *pantyhose*
paper कागज *kagaaj;*
~ napkins कागजी नैपकीन
kaagzee napkin
paracetamol पैरासीटामोल
paracetamol

paraffin पैराफिन *paraffin*
paralysis लकवा *lukwaa*
parcel पार्सल *parcel*
pardon? माफी? *maafi*
parents माता-पिता *mata-pita*
park पार्क *park*
park, to पार्क करना *park kurnaa*
parking lot पार्किंग *parking*
parking meter पार्किंग मीटर
parking meter
parliament building संसद भवन
sansad bhawan
partner (boyfriend/girlfriend)
सहयोगी *sahyogi*
parts पुर्जा *purjaa*
party पार्टी *party*
pass, to गुजरना *gujurnaa*
pass through, to से गुजरना
se gujurnaa
passport पासपोर्ट *passport*
pastry store पेस्ट्री की दुकान
pastry kee dukaan
patch, to पैबंद लगाना
paibund laganaa
patient (n.) धैर्यवान *dhairyawaan*
pavement, on the फर्श पर
phursh pur
pay, to भुगतान करना
bhugtaan karnaa
  ~ a fine जुर्माना देना *jurmaana dena*
pay phone पे फोन *pe phone*
payment भुगतान *bhugtaan*
peak शीर्ष *shirsh*

pearl मोती *moti*
pedestrian: ~ crossing पैदल
चलने वाला: पैदल चलने वालों
के लिए क्रॉसिंग *paidal chalne
waala: paidal chalne waalon ke liye
crossing;*
  ~ zone पैदल चलने वालों का क्षेत्र
paidal chalne waalon ka shetre
pen कलम *kalam*
pencil पेंसिल *pencil*
penknife कलम बनाने का चाकू
kalam banene kaa chaaku
people लोग *log*
pepper काली मिर्च *kaali mirch*
per: ~ day प्रति: प्रतिदिन
prati : pratidin;
  ~ hour प्रति घंटा *prati ghuntaa;*
  ~ night प्रति रात्रि *orati ratree;*
  ~ week प्रति सप्ताह *prati saptaah*
perhaps शायद *shaayad*
period (menstrual)
माहवारी *maahwaari*
  ~ pains माहवारी का दर्द
maahwaari ka dard
perm, to बाल घुंघराले कराना
baal ghungraale karnaa
petrol पेट्रोल *petrol;*
  ~ station पेट्रोल स्टेशन
petrol station
pewter काँसा *kaansaa*
pharmacy दवाखाना *dawakhaana*
phone: ~card फोन: फोन कार्ड
phone: phone card;
  ~ call फोन कॉल *phone call*

phone, to फोन करना
phone karma

photo: to take ~ चित्र: चित्र लेना
chitra: chitra lena

passport-size पासपोर्ट-आकार
चित्र *paasport-aakaar chitra*

photocopier फोटोकोपियर
photocopier

photographer फोटोग्राफर
photographer

phrase वाक्यखंड *vaakyakhund*

phrase book वाक्यखंड की पुस्तक
vaakyakhund kee pustak

pick someone up, to किसी को
लेना *kisi ko lena*

pick up, to किसी को लेना *kisi ko
lena*

picnic पिकनिक *picnic*;
~ area पिकनिक क्षेत्र *picnic
shetre*

piece हिस्सा *hissa*; **a piece of**
एक हिस्सा का *ek hissa ka*;

pill गोली *goli*

**Pill (contraceptive): to be on the
Pill** गोली: गोली के सहारे रहना
goli: goli ke sahare rehnaa

pillow तकिया *tukiyaa*;
~ case तकिया का खोल
tukiyaa kaa khol

pilot light पायलट लाइट *pilot light*

pink गुलाबी *gulaabi*

pipe (smoking) पाइप *pipe*

pitch (for camping) टेंट लगाना
tent lagaana

pizzeria पिज्जेरीया
pizzeria

place (n.) जगह *jagah*

place a bet, to दांव लगाना
daanv laganaa

plane जहाज *jahaj*

plans कल्पना *kalpanaa*

plant (n.) पौधा *paudha*

plastic: ~ bags प्लास्टिक:
प्लास्टिक बैग *plastic: plastic bag*;
~ wrap प्लास्टिक का आवरण
plastic kaa aavran

plate थाली *thaali*

platform प्लेटफॉर्म *platform*

platinum प्लेटिनम *platinum*

play, to (music) बजाना *bajana*
~ group खेल समूह *khel samooh*;
~ ground खेल का मैदान
khel kaa maidaan

playing field खेल का मैदान
khel kaa maidaan

playwright नाटककार
natakkaar

pleasant सुहाना *suhaana*

please कृपया *kripyaa*

plug प्लग *plug*

p.m. अपराह्न *apraahun*

pneumonia निमोनिया
pneumonia

point of interest आकर्षण बिंदु
aakurshun bindu

point to, to को दिखाना
ko dikhaana

poison ज़हर *zaher*

police पुलिस *police;*
~ **report** पुलिस रिपोर्ट *police report;*
~ **station** पुलिस स्टेशन *police station*

pollen count पराग गणना *parag gunnaa*

polyester पोलीस्टर *polyester*

pond तालाब *talaab*

pop (music) पॉप *pop*

popcorn पॉप कॉर्न *pop corn*

popular प्रसिद्ध *praseedh*

port बंदरगाह *bandurgaah*

porter (hotel) पोर्टर
porter (train station) कुली *kulee*

portion जगह *jagah*

possible: as soon as possible संभव: जितनी जल्दी संभव हो सके *sambhuv: jitnaa jaldee sambhuv ho sake*

possibly संभवत *sambhuvate*

post (mail) डाक *daak*
~ **office** डाकघर *daakghar;*
~ **box** पोस्ट बॉक्स *post box;*
~ **card** पोस्ट कार्ड *post card*

post, to डाक भेजना *daak bhejnaa*

postage डाक खर्च *daak khurch*

potato chips आलू चिप्स *aaloo chips*

potatoes आलू *aaloo*

pottery कुम्हारी विद्या *kumhaaree vidyaa*

pound (sterling) पाउंड *pound*

power: ~ **cut** बिजली: बिजली कटौती *bijlee: bijlee katautee;*
~ **points** बिजली के प्वाइंट *bijlee ke point*

pregnant, to be गर्भवती होना *garbhvati hona*

premium (gas/petrol) प्रीमियम *premium*

prescribe, to व्यवस्था करना *vyavusthaa karnaa*

prescription निर्देश *nirdesh*

present (gift) उपहार *uphaar*

press, to दबाना *dabanaa*

pretty सुंदर *sundur*

priest पुजारी *pujaari*

prison कारागार *karagaar*

probably शायद *shaayad*

produce store [grocer] किराने थक दुकान *kiraane kee dukaan*

program कार्यक्रम *karayakaram;*
~ **of events** कार्यक्रम की सूची *karayakaram kee soochi*

pronounce, to निर्णय सुनाना *nirnay sunnaa*

pub पब *pub*

public building सार्वजनिक भवन *saarvajanik bhawan*

pump पंप *pump*

puncture पंचर *puncture*

puppet show कठपुतली का खेल *kuthputlee kaa khel*

pure: pure cotton शुद्ध: शुद्ध सूती
shudh: shudh sooti
purple बैंगनी *bainganee*
purse पर्स *purse*
put: where can I put?
रखना: मैं कहाँ रख सकता हूँ?
rukhnaa: main kahan rukh saktaa hoon

Q

quality गुणवत्ता *gunvutta*
quantity मात्रा *maatraa*
quarter चौथाई *chauthai;*
  ~ past बजकर पंद्रह मिनट
  bujkur pandrah minute;
  ~ to बजने में पंद्रह मिनट *bajne mein pandrah minute*
queue, to पंक्ति में खड़े होना
panktee mein khade hona
quick तेज *tej*
quickest: what's the quickest way? सबसे तेज: सबसे तेज तरीका क्या है? *sabse tej: sabse tarikaa kya hai*
quickly तेजी से *teji se*
quiet शांत *shaant*
quieter अधिक शांति *adhik shaantee*

R

race track [racecourse] रेसकोर्स *race course*
racket रैकेट *racket*
railway रेल *rail*
rain, to बारिश होना *bearish hona*

raincoat बरसाती *barsaatee*
rape बलात्कार *balatkaar*
rapids झरना *jhurnaa*
rare अतुल्य *atulyaa*
rash चकत्ता *chuktaa*
rather प्राय *prayah*
razor रेजर *razor;*
  ~ blades रेजर ब्लेड *razor blade*
reading पढ़ना *padhnaa*
ready तैयार *tayaar*
real वास्तविक *vastaavik*
really? सचमुच? *suchmuch*
receipt रसीद *raseed*
reception (desk) स्वागत *swagat*
receptionist रिसेप्शनिस्ट *receptionist*
recommend, to सलाह देना *salaah dena;*
  can you recommend?
  क्या आप सलाह दे सकते हैं?
  kya aap salaah de sakte hain;
  what do you recommend?
  आप क्या सलाह दे सकते हैं?
  aap kya salaah de sakte hain
red लाल *laal;*
  ~ wine रेड वइन *red wine*
reduction कमी *kami*
refreshments जलपान *jalpaan*
refrigerator रेफ्रिजरेटर *refrigerator*
refund वापसी *waapsi*
regards: give my regards to
आदर: को मेरा आदर देना
aadur ko mera aadur dena
region क्षेत्र *shetre*

registered mail पंजीकृत मेल
panjeekrit mail

registration form पंजीकरण फॉर्म
panjeekaran form

registration number (car)
पंजीकरण संख्या *panjeekaran
sankhya*

regular नियमित *niyamit*

religion धर्म *dharma*

remember: I don't remember
याद करना: मुझे याद नहीं
yaad kurnaa: mujhe yaad nahin

rent, to ~ out किराया, किराए पर
देना *kiraaya, kiraaye pur dena;*
I'd like to rent मैं किराए पर
लेना चाहूंगा *main kiraay pur lena
chahoongaa*

repair, to मरम्मत करना
murummut karnaa

repairs मरम्मत *murummut*

repeat, to दोहराना *dorahnaa;*
please repeat that
कृपया उसे दोहराएं *kripyaa use
dohraaye*

replacement बदल *badal;*
~ part बदला हुआ पुर्जा
badlaa hua purjaa

report, to बताना *bataana*

require, to आकांक्षा करना
aakaanshaa karnaa

required, to be आकांक्षा होना
aakaanshaa hona

reservation आरक्षण
aarakshun

reservations desk आरक्षण डेस्क
aarukshun desk

reserve, to आरक्षण करना
aarukshun **kurnaa; I'd like to
reserve**
मैं आरक्षित करना चाहूंगा
main aarakshit karnaa chahoongaa

rest, to आराम करना *aaraam
kurnaa*

restaurant रेस्टोरेंट *restaurant*

retail खुदरा *khudra*

retired, to be अवकाश प्राप्त होना
avkaash prapt hona

return (adj.) वापसी *waapsee*
~ ticket वापसी टिकट
waapsee ticket

return, to वापस होना *waapus
hona*

reverse the charges, to शुल्क
उल्टा कर देना *shulk ulta kur dena*

revolting राजद्रोही *raajdrohi*

rheumatism गठिया *guthiyaa*

rib पसली *puslee*

rice चावल *chaawal*

right (direction) : on the ~ दाएं:
दाहिने की ओर *daanyan: daahine
kee aur*

right (correct) ठीक *theek;*
that's ~ यह ठीक है
yeh theek hai

right of way रास्ते पर अधिकार
raaste pur adhikaar

ring अंगूठी *angoothi*

rip-off (n.) डकैती *dacaitee*

river नदी *nadi;*

~ **cruise** नदी क्रूज़ *nadi cruise*

road सड़क *sadak;*

~ **map** सड़क मानचित्र *sadak maanchitra;*

~ **closed** सड़क बंद *sadak bund*

robbed, to be लूट लिया जाना *loot liya jaana*

robbery डकैती *dacaitee*

rock music रॉक संगीत *rock sangeet*

rolls रौल्स *rolls*

romantic रोमांटिक *romantic*

roof छत *chhut*

~-**rack** रूफ रैक *roof rack*

room कमरा *kumara;*

~ **service** रूम सेवा *room seva*

rope रस्सी *rassi*

round गोलाई *golaai*

~ **neck** गोल गला *gol gala*

round (of golf) राउंड *round*

round-trip वापसी *waapsee*

~ **ticket** वापसी का टिकट *waapsee kaa ticket*

route मार्ग *marg*

rubbish कूड़ा-करकट *kooda-kurkut*

rude, to be असभ्य होना *asabhya hona*

ruins खंडहर *khundhur*

run: ~ **into** भिड़ंत *bhidant*

~ **out** समाप्त होना *samapt hona*

running shoes दौड़ने वाला जूता *daudne waala jota*

rush hour भीड़ वाला समय *bheed waala samay*

S

safari सफारी *safari*

safari park सफारी पार्क *safari park*

safe (n.) तिजोरी *tijoree*

safe (adj.) सुरक्षित *surukshit*

to feel ~ सुरक्षित महसूस करना *surukshit mehsoos karnaa*

safety सुरक्षा *surukshaa;*

~ **pins** सेफ्टी पिन *safety pin*

salad सलाद *salad*

sales बिक्री *bikree;*

~ **tax** बिक्री कर *bikree kar*

salt नमक *namak*

salty नमकीन *namkeen*

same समान *samaan*

sand रेत *rait*

sandals सैंडल *sandal*

sandwich सैंडविच *sandwich*

sandy रेतीला *raiteela*

sanitary napkins [towels] तौलिया *tauliyaa*

satellite TV सेटेलाइट टीवी *satellite TV*

satin साटन *satin*

satisfied: I'm not satisfied with this संतुष्ट: मैं इससे संतुष्ट नहीं हूँ *santusht: main isse santusht nahin hoon*

Saturday शनिवार *shanivaar*

sauce चटनी *chutney*

saucepan सॉस पैन *saucepan*

sauna सौना *sauna*
sausages सॉसेज़ *sausages*
say: how do you say?
कहना: आप कैसे कहते हैं?
kehna: aap kaise kehte hain
scan (computer) स्कैन (कंप्यूटर)
scan (computer)
scarf दुपट्टा *dupatta*
scenic route दर्शनीय रास्ता
darshiniye raasta
scheduled flight पूर्वनिर्धारित
उड़ान *purvnidhaarit udaan*
school विद्यालय *vidyalaya*
sciatica साइटिका *saitika*
scissors कैंची *kainchi*
scooter स्कूटर *scooter*
screwdriver स्क्रू ड्राइवर
screwdriver
sea समुद्र *samudra*
seafront सी-फ्रंट *sea-front*
seasick: I feel ~ सी-सिकनेस: मैं
सी-सिकनेस महसूस कर रहा हूँ
*sea sickness: main sea sickness
mehsoos kur raha hoon*
season ticket सीज़न टिकट
season ticket
seasoning सीज़निंग
seasoning
seat बैठने की जगह *baithne kee
jagah*
is this seat taken? क्या यह सीट
भरी है? *kya yeh seat bhari hai*
second द्वितीय *dweeteye;*
~ **class (ticket)**

द्वितीय श्रेणी (टिकट)
dweeteye shrenee (ticket);
~**-hand** पुराना *puraana*
secretary सचिव *sachiv*
sedative शांतिकर *shaantikar*
see, to देखना *dekhnaa*
see you soon! फिर मिलते हैं!
phir milte hain
self-employed, to be
स्व-रोजगार होना
swa-rozgaar hona
self-service स्व-सेवा *swa-sewa*
send, to भेजना *bhejnaa*
senior citizen वरिष्ठ नागरिक
varisht naagrik
separated, to be
अलग होना *alag hona*
separately अलग अलग
lag alag
September सितम्बर *sitambar*
serious(ly) गम्भीरतापूर्वक
gambhirtaapurvuk
served, to be परोसना *parosnaa*
service सेवा *sewa*
is service included?
क्या सेवा शुल्क शामिल है?
kya sewa shulk shaamil hai
serviette सर्विएट *serviette*
set menu मेनु सेट करें *menu set
karen*
sex (act) सेक्स *sex*
shade (color) रंग *rang*
shady छायादार *chayaadaar*
shallow छिछला *chichlaa*

shampoo शैंपू *shampoo;*
~ and set धुँपू शैंपू सेट करवाना
shampoo aur set karnaa
shape आकार *aakaar*
share, to हिस्सेदारी करना
hissedaari karma
sharp items नुकीला सामान
nukeela samaan
shaving: ~ brush शेविंग: शेविंग
ब्रश *shaving: shaving brush;*
~ cream शेविंग क्रीम *shaving
cream*
she वह *weh*
sheet *(bedding)* चादर
chaadur
ship जहाज *jahaj*
shirt कमीज *kameez*
shock *(electric)* झटका *jhutka*
shoe repair जूता मरम्मत
jota murummut
shoe store जूते की दुकान
joote kee dukaan
shoes जूते *joote*
shop दुकान *dukaan;*
~ assistant दुकान में सहायक
dukaan mein sahayak
shopping: ~ area
खरीदारी: खरीदारी क्षेत्र
khareedari: khareedaari shetre;
~ basket खरीदारी वाली टोकरी
khareedari waali tokree;
~mall [centre] शॉपिंग माल
shopping mall
~ trolley शॉपिंग ट्रॉली

shopping trolley;
to go ~ खरीदारी के लिए जाना
khareedaari ke liye jaana
short छोटा *chotaa;* **~-sighted**
सुक्ष्म दृष्टि *suksham drishti*
shorts शॉर्ट्स *shorts*
shoulder *da/kk kandha*
shovel बेलचा *belcha*
show, to दिखाना *dikhaana*
shower शावर *shower*
shut बंद करना *bund karnaa;*
when do you shut?
आप कब बंद करते हैं?
aap kun bund karte hain
sick: I'm going to be sick
बीमार: मैं बीमार होने वाला हूँ
*bimaar: main bimaar hone waala
hoon*
side (of road) किनारा *kinaara*
~ street किनारे वाली गली
kinaare waali ghadi
side order साइड ऑर्डर
side order
sides (hair) बगलें *buglein*
sights दृश्य *drishya*
sightseeing: ~ tour
दृश्यावलोकन: दृश्यावलोकन
भ्रमण *drishyavlokan:
drishyaavlokan;*
to go ~ दृश्यावलोकन के लिए
जाना *drishyaavlokan ke liye jaana*
sign संकेत *sanket*
signpost मार्ग-सूचक स्तंभ
marg-soochak stumbh

silk रेशम *reshum*
silver चांदी *chaandi;*
 ~-plate चांदी की थाली
 chaandi kee thaili
singer गायक *gaayak*
single एकल *ekal*
 ~ room सिंगल कमरा *single kamraa;* **~ ticket** सिंगल टिकट
 single ticket; **to be ~** अविवाहित
 होना *avivaahit hona*
sink डूबना *doobnaa*
sister बहन *bahan*
sit, to बैठना *baithnaa*
sit down, बैठ जाओ *baith jao;*
 please कृपया *kripyaa*
size आकार *aakaar*
skin त्वचा *twacha*
skirt स्कर्ट *skirt*
sleep, to सोना *sona*
sleeping: ~ bag सोना: सोने वाला
 बैग *sona: sone waala bag;*
 ~ car शयनयान कार *shayanyaan car;*
 ~ pill नींद की गोली *neend kee goli*
sleeve बाजू *baaju*
slice टुकड़ा *tukdaa*
slippers चप्पल *chappal*
slow धीमा *dheema;*
 to be ~ धीमा चलना *dheema chulna*
slow down! धीमे हो जाओ!
 dheeme ho jao
slowly धीमे से *dheeme se*

small छोटा *chota;* **~ change (coins)** छोटे खुल्ले *chote khulle*
smell: there's a bad smell
 गंध: कुछ बदबू है *gandh: kuch badboo hai*
smoke, to धूम्रपान करना
 dhrumpaan karnaa
smoking धूम्रपान *dhrumpaan*
snack bar स्नैक बार *snack bar*
snacks स्नैक *snack*
sneakers जूता *jota*
snorkel स्नोर्केल *snorkel*
snow, to बर्फ पड़ना *burf padnaa*
soap साबुन *saabun*
soap powder साबुन का पाउडर
 saabun kaa powder
soccer फुटबॉल *football*
socket सॉकेट *socket*
socks जुर्राबें *juraabe*
soft drink सॉफ्ट ड्रिंक *soft drink*
solarium सोलेरियम *solarium*
sole (shoes) सोल *sole*
soluble aspirin घुलनशील एस्प्रीन
 ghulnashil aspirin
some कुछ *kuch*
someone कोई *koi*
something कुछ *kuch*
sometimes कई बार *kai baar*
son बेटा *beta*
soon जल्दी *jaldee*
soon: as soon as possible
 जल्दी: जितनी जल्दी संभव हो
 सके
 jaldee: jitni jaldee sambhav ho sake

sore: it's ~ व्रण: व्रण है *vrana:*
vrana hai; **~ throat** कंठव्रण
kanthavrana

sorry! क्षमा! *shama*

sort क्रम *krum*

soul music जीवन संगीत
jeevan sangeet

sour खट्टा *khutta*

south दक्षिण *dakshin*

South Africa दक्षिण अफ़्रीका
dakshin africa

souvenir स्मारिका *smaarikaa;*
~ store स्मारिका की दुकान
smaarikaa kee dukaan

soy sauce सोयाबीन की चटनी
soyabean kee chutney

space स्थान *sthaan*

spare *(extra)* अतिरिक्त *atirikt*

speak, to बोलना *bolnaa;*
~ to से बोलना *se bolnaa;*

do you speak English? क्या आप
अंग्रेज़ी बोलते हैं? *kya aap angreji*
bolte hain

special: ~ delivery
विशेष: विशेष वितरण
vishesh: vishesh vitrun;
~ rate विशेष दर *vishesh dur*

specialist विशेषज्ञ *visheshyagya*

specimen नमूना *namoona*

speed, to गति बढ़ाना *gati*
badhnaa

spend, to खर्च करना *khurch*
karnaa

spicy मसालेदार *masaledaar*

sponge स्पंज *sponge*

spoon चम्मच *chummuch*

sport खेल *khel*

sporting goods store
खेल के सामान की दुकान
khel ke samay kee dukaan

sports खेल *khel;*
~ club स्पोर्ट्स क्लब *sports club;*
~ ground खेल का मैदान
khel kaa maidaan

sprained, to be
मोच आना *moch aana*

spring वसंत *vasant*

square चौकोर *chaukaur*

stadium स्टेडियम *stadium*

staff कर्मचारी *karamchaari*

stain धब्बा *dhubba*

stainless steel
स्टेनलेस स्टील *stainless steel*

stairs सीढ़ियाँ *seedheeyaan*

stamp टिकट *ticket;*
~ machine टिकट की मशीन
ticket kee machine

stand in line, to पंक्ति में खड़ा
होना *punktee mein khadaa hona*

standby ticket वैकल्पिक टिकट
vaikulpik ticket

start, to आरंभ करना *aarambh*
karnaa

statement (legal) वक्तव्य
vaktavya

station स्टेशन *station*

statue मूर्ति *murtee*

stay *(n.)* पड़ाव *padaav*

stay, to ठहरना *thuharnaa*
steak house मांस खाने की जगह
maans khaane ki jagah
sterilizing solution
स्टेरिलाइजेशन सॉल्यूशन
sterilization solution
stiff neck गर्दन में अकड़न
gardan mein akdun
still: I'm still waiting अभी तक:
मैं अभी तक इंतजार कर रहा हूँ
*abhi tuk: main abhi tuk intezaar kar
raha hoon*
sting डंक *dunk*
stockings मोजा *mauza*
stolen, to be चुरा लिया गया
churaa liya hai
stomach पेट *pet;*
~ ache पेट दर्द *pet dard*
stool मल *mul*
stop (bus) पड़ाव *padaav*
stop (at), to पर रुकना *pur ruknaa*
store दुकान *dukaan*
stormy, to be तूफानी होना
toofaani hona
stove चूल्हा *chulhaa*
straight ahead सीधे सामने
seedhe saamne
strained muscle
मोच वाली मांसपेशी
mooch waali maanspeshi
strange अजीबोगरीब
ajeebogareeb
straw (drinking) स्ट्रॉ *straw*
strawberry स्ट्रॉबेरी *strawberry*

stream धारा *dhaara*
strong शक्तिशाली *shakteeshaali*
student छात्र *chhatra*
study, to अध्ययन करना
adhyan kurnaa
style शैली *shaili*
subtitled, to be सबटाइटल्ड होना
subtitled hona
subway मेट्रो *metro*
~ station मेट्रो स्टेशन
metro station
sugar चीनी *cheenee*
suggest, to सुझाव देना
sujhaav dena
suit उपयुक्त करना *upyukt karma*
suitable for उपयुक्त होना
upyukt hona
summer गर्मी *garmi*
sun block सन ब्लॉक *sun block*
sunbathe, to
धूप सेंकना *dhoop sainknaa*
sunburn सन बर्न *sun burn*
Sunday रविवार *raviwaar*
sunglasses धूप का चश्मा
dhoop ka chushma
sunscreen सन-स्क्रीन *sun-screen*
sunshade सन शेड *sun shade*
sunstroke सूर्याघात *suryaghaat*
super (gas/petrol) सुपर *super*
superb उत्तम *uttam*
supermarket सुपरमार्केट
supermarket
supervision पर्यवेक्षण
paryaveshun

supplement परिशिष्ट *parishisht*
suppositories सपोज़िट्री
suppository
sure: are you sure?
विश्वस्त: क्या आप विश्वस्त हैं?
vishvust: kya aap vishvust hai
surfboard सर्फ बोर्ड *surf board*
surname उपनाम *upnaam*
sweater स्वेटर *sweater*
sweatshirt स्वेट शॉर्ट *sweatshirt*
sweet मीठा *meetha*
sweets मिठाई *mithai*
swelling सूजन *soojun*
swim, to तैरना *tairnaa*
swimming तैराकी *tairaaki;*
    ~ pool स्वीमिंग पूल
    swimming pool;
    ~ trunks स्वीमिंग ट्रंक
    swimming trunk
swimsuit स्वीमिंग सूट *swimming
suit*
switch स्विच *switch*
swollen, to be सूज जाना *sooch
jaana*
symptoms लक्षण *lakshun*
synagogue
    यहूदियों का पूजा के लिए जमघट
    *yahoodiyon kaa pooja ke liye
    jumghut*
synthetic सिंथेटिक *synthetic*

T

T-shirt टी शर्ट *t-shirt*
table टेबल *table*

tablet टेबलेट *tablet*
take, to लेना *lena;*
I'll take it मैं इसे लूंगा
    main ise loonga;
    ~ out निकलवाना *nikalwaanaa*
    ~ photographs, to फोटो खींचना
    photo kheechnaa
taken व्यस्त *vyast*
talk, to बात करना *baat kurnaa*
tall लंबा *lumba*
tampons टैम्पन *tampon*
tan त्वचा को धूप से भूरा करना
    twacha ko dhoop se bhoora rakhna
tap टोंटी *tontee*
taxi टैक्सी *taxi;*
    ~ stand [rank] टैक्सी स्टैंड *taxi
    stand*
tea चाय *chai;* **~ bags** टी बैग *tea
bag;*
    ~ towel टी टॉवेल *tea towel*
teacher शिक्षक *shikshak*
team टीम *team*
teaspoon चम्मच *chummuch*
teddy bear टेडी बियर *teddy bear*
telephone टेलीफोन *telephone;*
    ~ booth टेलीफोन बूथ
    telephone booth;
    ~ call टेलीफोन कॉल *telephone
    call;* **~ directory** टेलीफोन
    डायरेक्ट्री *telephone directory;*
    ~ number टेलीफोन नंबर
    telephone number
telephone, to टेलीफोन करना
    telephone kurnaa

temperature तापमान *taapmaan*

temporarily अस्थाई रूप से
asthaai roop se

ten thousand दस हज़ार
dus hazaar

tennis टेनिस *tennis*;
~ court टेनिस कोर्ट *tennis court*

tent टेंट *tent*;
~ pegs टेंट खूँटी *tent khoontee*;
~ pole टेंट खंबा *tent khumbaa*

terrible भयंकर *bhayankar*

terrific शानदार *shaandaar*

tetanus टेटनिस *tetanus*

thali थाली *thali*

thank you धन्यवाद *dhanyawaad*

that one वह *weh*

that's all अब बस *ab bus*

theater नाट्यशाला *natyashaala*

theft चोरी *chori*

their(s) उनका *unka*

theme park थीम पार्क *theme park*

then तब *tub*

there वहाँ *wahan*

there is वहाँ है *wahan hai*

there are वहाँ हैं *wahan hai*

thermometer थर्मामीटर
thermometer

thermos flask थर्मस फ्लास्क
thermos flask

these ये *yeh*

they वे *weh*

thief चोर *chor*

thigh जांघ *jaangh*

thin पतला *putlaa*

think: ~ about it
सोचना: इस बारे में सोचें *sochnaa:
is bare mein sochen*; **what do you
~ of ..?** आप ... के बारे में क्या
सोचते हैं? *aap ... ke bare mein kya
sochte hain*

I think (feel) मैं विचार
main vichaar

I think (it seems) मेरे विचार से
mere vichaar se

third तृतीय *triteeye*; **~ party**
तृतीय पक्ष *triteeye paksh*;

insurance बीमा *bema*;

third, एक तिहाई *ek tihai*

thirsty: I am thirsty
प्यास: मैं प्यासा हूँ
pyaas: main pyaasa hoon

this यह *yeh*; **~ one** यह *yeh*

those वे *weh*

thousand हज़ार *hazaar*

throat गला *gala*

thrombosis थ्रॉम्बोसिस
thrombosis

through द्वारा *dwaara*

thumb अंगूठा *angootha*

Thursday गुरुवार *guruvaar*

ticket टिकट *ticket*
~ office टिकट कार्यालय
ticket karayalaya

tie टाई *tie*

tiger बाघ *baagh*

tight तंग *tung*

tights टाइट्स *tights*

till receipt रसीद *raseed*

time समय *samay;* **on ~** समय पर *samay pur;* **free ~** ख़ाली समय *khaali samay;* **... times a day** दिन में ... बार *din mein ... baar*

timetable समय-सारणी *samay-saarni*

tin टिन *tin;*
~ **opener** टिन ओपनर *tin opener*

tire टायर (कार) *tire (car)*

tired: I'm tired थकान: मैं थका हूँ *thakaan: main thakaa hoon*

tissues टिश्यू *tissue*

to तक *tuk*

tobacco तम्बाकू *tumbakoo*

tobacconist तम्बाकू की दुकान *tumbakoo kee dukaan*

today आज *aaj*

toe पंजा *punja*

tofu सोयाबीन का पनीर *soyabean ka paneer*

together साथ साथ *saath saath*

toilet शौचालय *shauchalaya;*
~ **paper** टॉयलेट पेपर *toilet paper*

tomorrow कल *kul*

tongue जीभ *jheebh*

tonight आज रात *aaj raat*

tonsilitis टांसीलाइटिस *tonsillitis*

tonsils टांसिल *tonsil*

too भी *bhi;*
~ **much** बहुत ज्यादा *bahut zyaadaa*

tooth दांत *daant;*
~ **brush** टूथ ब्रश *tooth brush;*
~ **ache** दांत का दर्द *daant kaa dard;*
~ **paste** टूथ पेस्ट *tooth paste*

top शीर्ष *shirsh*

torch टॉर्च *torch*

torn: this is torn फट जाना: यह फट गया है *phut jaana: yeh phut gaya hai*

tough कड़ा *kada*

tour भ्रमण *bhraman;*
~ **guide** भ्रमण गाइड *bhraman guide;*
~ **operator** भ्रमण संचालक *brahman sanchaluk*

tourist सैलानी *sailaani*

tow truck खींचने वाला ट्रक *kheenchne waala truck*

towards की दिशा में *kee disha mein*

towel तौलिया *tauliya*

tower मीनार *minaar*

town शहर *sheher*
~ **hall** टाउन हॉल *town hall*

toy खिलौना *khilonaa;*
~ **store** खिलौनों की दुकान *khilonon kee dukaan*

traditional परंपरागत *paramparagat*

traffic यातायात *yatayaat;*
~ **jam** यातायात जाम *yatayaat jam;*

trail सामान्य पथ *saamanya path*

trailer ट्रेलर *trailer*

train ट्रेन *train;*

~ **station** ट्रेन स्टेशन
train station

training shoes प्रशिक्षण के लिए
जूते *prakshishun ke liye joote*

tram ट्राम *tram*

transfer स्थानांतरण *sthanataran*

transit, in संक्रमण में *sankraman mein*

translate, to अनुवाद करें
anuvaad karen

translation अनुवाद *anuvaad*

translator अनुवादक *anuvaaduk*

trash कूड़ा *kooda;*

~ **cans** कूड़ा का डब्बा *kooda kaa dubba*

travel:

~ **agency** पर्यटन: ट्रेवल एजेंसी
paryatun: travel agency;

~ **sickness** यात्रा संबंधित बीमारी
yatraa sambundhit bimaari

traveler's check [cheque]
ट्रेवलर चेक *traveler check*

tray ट्रे *tray*

tree पेड़ *per*

trim ट्रीम करवाना *trim kurwanaa*

trip यात्रा *yatraa*

have a good trip आपकी यात्रा
सुखद हो *aapki yaatra sukhud ho*

trolley ट्रॉली *trolley*

trousers पतलून *putloon*

truck ट्रक *truk*

true: that's ~ सच: वह सच है
such: weh such hai

that's not ~ वह सच नहीं है
weh such nahin hai

try on, to प्रयत्न करें
puryatun karen

Tuesday मंगलवार
mangalwaar

tumor ट्यूमर *tumor*

tunnel सुरंग *surung*

turn, to मुड़ना *moodhnaa;*

~ **down** कम करें *kum karen*

~ **off** बंद करें *bund karen;*

~ **on** चालू करें *chaaloo karen;*

~ **up** अधिक करें *adhik aren*

turning मुड़ना *moodhna*

TV टीवी *TV*

tweezers ट्वीज़र *tweezer*

twice दोबारा *dobaaraa*

twin bed टि्वन बेड *twin bed*

twist: I've twisted my ankle
ऐंठन: मेरे पैर में ऐंठन हो गई है
ainthun: mere paer mein ainthun ho gayi hai

two-door car दो दरवाजे वाली कार
do durwaaje waali car

type प्रकार *prakaar*

what type? किस प्रकार?
kis prakaar

typical आदर्शभूत *adurshbhoot*

tyre टायर *tyre*

U

ugly बदसूरत *badsoorat*

ulcer नासूर *naasoor*

umbrella छाता *chaataa*

uncle चाचा *chacha*

unconscious, to be बेहोश होना
behosh hona

under uhps *neeche*

underdone अधपका *adhpaka*

underpants अंतर्वस्त्र *anturvastra*

underpass भूमिगत पारपथ
bhoomigut paarpath

understand, to समझना
samjhnaa

do you understand?
क्या तुम समझे?
kya tum samjhe

I don't understand मैं समझा नहीं।
main samjha nahin

undress, to कपड़े उतारना
kapde uttarnaa

uneven असमतल *asamtul*

unfortunately दुर्भाग्यवश
durbhayavush

uniform यूनिफॉर्म *uniform*

unit इकाई *ikaai*

United States अमेरिका *america*

unlimited mileage माइलेज
mileage

unlock, to खोलना *kholnaa*

unpleasant अप्रिय *apriye*

unscrew, to खोलना *kholnaa*

until तब तक *tub tuk*

up to तक *tuk*

upset stomach पेट खराब
चमज ीतंड्

upstairs ऊपरी मंजिल *upree
manzil*

urine पेशाब *peshaab*

use, to इस्तेमाल करना
istemaal karnaa

use: for my personal use
इस्तेमाल: मेरे निजी इस्तेमाल
के लिए
istemaal: mere niji istemaal ke liye

V

V-neck वी-गला *V-gala*

vacant खाली *khaali*

vacation, on छुट्टी पर *chutti pur*

vaccinated against, to be का
टीका लगाना *ka tikka lagana*

vaginal infection योनि का
संक्रमण *yoni kaa sankramun*

valet service वैले सेवा *valet sewa*

valid मान्य *manya*

validate, to प्रमाणित करना
pramanit kurnaa

valley घाटी *ghaati*

valuable मूल्यवान *mulyavaan*

value मूल्य *mulya*

valve वॉल्व *valve*

vanilla वनीला *vanilla*

VAT वैट *VAT;*

~ receipt वैट रसीद *VAT raseed*

vegan, to be शाकाहारी होना
shakahaari hona

vegetables सब्जियां *subjiyan*

vegetarian शाकाहारी *shaakaahaari*
to be शाकाहारी होना
shaakahari hona

vehicle registration document
वाहन रजिस्ट्रेशन कागजात
waahan registration kagzaat

vein नस *nus*

venereal disease यौन रोग
yon rog

ventilator रोशनदार *roshundaan*

very बहुत *bahut*

video: ~ game वीडियो: वीडियो
खेल *video: video khel;*
~ recorder वीडियो रिकॉर्डर
video recorder

view: with a view of the sea
दृश्य: समुद्र का दृश्य के साथ
drishya: samudra kaa drishya ke saath

viewpoint दृश्यावलोकन स्थल
drishyavalokun sthul

village गांव *gaon*

vinaigrette विनाएग्रेट *vinaigrette*

vineyard/winery अंगूर का
बगीचा/वाइनरी *angoor ka bagichaa*

visa वीसा *visa*

visit (n.) आगमन *aagmun*

visit, to (v.) मिलना *milnaa*

visiting hours दर्शन करने का
समय *darshan karne kaa samay*

vitamin tablets विटामिन टेबलेट
vitamin tablet

volleyball वॉलीबॉल *volleyball*

voltage वॉल्टेज *voltage*

vomit, to उल्टी करना *ulte kurnaa*

W

wait (for), to प्रतीक्षा करना
prateeksha kurna

wait! रुको! *ruko*

waiter वेटर *waiter*

waiting room प्रतीक्षालय
prateekshaalaya

waitress वेट्रेस *waitress*

wake, to जगाना *jaganaa*

wake-up call वेक-अप कॉल
wake-up call

walk (n.) पैदलचालन
paidulchaalun;
walking route पैदल चालन
रास्ता *paidal chaalan raastaa*

wallet बटुआ *batuaa*

war memorial युद्ध स्मारक
yudh samaaruk

ward (hospital) वार्ड *ward*

warm गर्म *garam*

washbasin वोश बेसिन *washbasin*

washing: ~ machine
वॉशिंग: वॉशिंग मशीन
washing: washing machine;
~ powder वॉशिंग पाउडर
washing powder

washing-up liquid
धुलाई वाला द्रव
dhulaai wala drava

wasp बर्रे *burre*

watch ध्यान देना *dhyaan dena*

water पानी *paani;*
~ bottle पानी की बोतल
paani kee bottle;
~ heater पानी गर्म करने वाला
paani garam karne waala;

~ skis वाटर स्की *water ski*

waterfall जलप्रपात *julprapaat*

waterproof वाटरप्रूफ़ *waterproof*

~ jacket वाटर-प्रूफ़ जैकेट
water-proof jacket

wave लहर *laher*

waxing वेक्सिंग *waxing*

way तरफ *taraf*

on the की तरफ *kee taraf*

we हमलोग *humlog*

wear, to पहनना *pehennaa*

weather मौसम *mausam;*

~ forecast मौसम पूर्वानुमान
mausam purvaaun

wedding शादी *shaadi;*

~ ring शादी की अंगूठी *shaadi
kee angoothi*

Wednesday बुधवार *budhwaar*

week सप्ताह *week*

weekend: on [at] the

~ साप्ताहांत: साप्ताहांत पर
saptahaant: saptahaant pur;

~ rate साप्ताहांत दर *saptahaant
dur*

weight: my weight is
वजन: मेरा वजन है
vajan: mera vajan hai

welcome to में स्वागत है
mein swaagat hai

well-done *(meat)* बहुत अच्छा
bahut achaa

west पश्चिमी *paschimi*

wetsuit वेट सूट *wet suit*

what: what time? क्या: कितने
समय? *kya : kitne samay*

what's the time? कितने बजे हैं?
kitne baje hain

what kind of? किस तरह का?
kis tarah kaa

wheelchair व्हील चेयर
wheel chair

when? कब? *kub*

where? कहाँ? *kahan*

where are you from?
आप कहाँ से आए हैं?
aap kahan se aaye hain

where is the? कहाँ है? *kahan hai*

where were you born?
आप का जन्म कहाँ हुआ था?
aapkaa janam kahan hua tha

which? कौन सा? *kaun saa*

white सफेद *white*

wine मदिरा *madiraa*

who? कौन? *kaun*

whose? किसका? *kiskaa*

why? क्यों? *kyon*

wide चौड़ा *chaudaa*

wife पत्नी *patni*

WiFi वाईफाई *wifi*

wildlife वन जीवन *vun jeevan*

windbreaker विंडब्रेकर
windbreaker

window खिड़की *khirkee;*

~ seat खिड़की के पास वाली
सीट *khirkee ke paas waali seat*

windscreen विंडस्क्रीन *windscreen*

windy, to be हवादार होना
hawadaar hona
wine मदिरा *madiraa;*
~ list मदिरा सूची *madiraa soochi*
winter जाड़ा *jaadaa*
wishes: best wishes
शुभकामनाएं: *shubhkaamnaay*
with साथ *saath*
withdraw, to निकालना
nikaalnaa
within में *mein*
without बिना *bina*
witness गवाह *gawah*
wood जंगल *jungle*
wool ऊन *oon*
work: ~ for काम: के लिए काम
kaam: ke liye kaam
it doesn't work यह काम नहीं
करता *yeh kaam nahin kurta*
worse बदतर *budtur*
worst सबसे बुरा *sabse buraa*
wound घाव *ghaav*
write down, to लिखना *likhnaa*
wrong गलत *galat*
~ number गलत नंबर *galat*

number
to be ~ गलत होना *galat hona*
there's something wrong with
के साथ कुछ गड़बड़ है
ke saath kuch gadbad hai

X
X-ray एक्स रे *X-ray*
Y
yacht याॅट *yacht*
year साल *saal*
yellow पीला *peela*
yes हां *haan*
yesterday कल *kul*
yogurt दही *dahi*
you (formal) आप *aap*
(informal) तुम *tum*
young जवान *jawaan*
your(s) *(pl.)* आपका *aapkaa (sing.)*
आप लोगों का *aap logon kaa*
youth hostel यूथ हॉस्टल *youth hostel*

Z
zero शून्य *hunya*
zip(per) जिपर *zipper*